Aurelia

Robert Thomas

A Samuel French Acting Edition

SAMUELFRENCH-LONDON.CO.UK
SAMUELFRENCH.COM

Copyright © 1976 by Tudor Gates
All Rights Reserved

AURELIA is fully protected under the copyright laws of the British Commonwealth, including Canada, the United States of America, and all other countries of the Copyright Union. All rights, including professional and amateur stage productions, recitation, lecturing, public reading, motion picture, radio broadcasting, television and the rights of translation into foreign languages are strictly reserved.

ISBN 978-0-573-01593-9

www.samuelfrench-london.co.uk

www.samuelfrench.com

FOR AMATEUR PRODUCTION ENQUIRIES

UNITED KINGDOM AND WORLD EXCLUDING NORTH AMERICA

plays@SamuelFrench-London.co.uk

020 7255 4302/01

Each title is subject to availability from Samuel French,

depending upon country of performance.

CAUTION: Professional and amateur producers are hereby warned that *AURELIA* is subject to a licensing fee. Publication of this play does not imply availability for performance. Both amateurs and professionals considering a production are strongly advised to apply to the appropriate agent before starting rehearsals, advertising, or booking a theatre. A licensing fee must be paid whether the title is presented for charity or gain and whether or not admission is charged.

The professional rights in this play are controlled by Eric Glass Ltd, 25 Ladbroke Crescent, London W11 1PS.

No one shall make any changes in this title for the purpose of production. No part of this book may be reproduced, stored in a retrieval system, or transmitted in any form, by any means, now known or yet to be invented, including mechanical, electronic, photocopying, recording, videotaping, or otherwise, without the prior written permission of the publisher. No one shall upload this title, or part of this title, to any social media websites.

The right of Robert Thomas to be identified as author of this work has been asserted by him in accordance with Section 77 of the Copyright, Designs and Patents Act 1988

CHARACTERS

Aurelia
Isabel
Lady Chalmont
Vera, her housekeeper-companion
Mercer
A Visitor

The action of the play takes place in the drawing-room of Lady Chalmont's house on the edge of a Cotswold village

ACT I
   Scene 1   An afternoon in March
   Scene 2   About noon, four days later
   Scene 3   Night, four days later
   Scene 4   Morning, several days later

ACT II
   Scene 1   Immediately following
   Scene 2   Several nights later
   Scene 3   One hour later

Time – the present

ACT I

Scene 1

The drawing-room of Lady Chalmont's house on the edge of a Cotswold village. A dreary late afternoon in March

The old house has been tastefully converted, some interior walls having been removed to make a large main living-room which serves as a gallery for Lady Chalmont's collection of paintings. Doors L *and* R *lead respectively to the kitchen and the dining-room. The open plan of the room reveals the polished wood staircase which leads to the floor above. There are picture windows at the rear looking out to the garden. The furnishings are comfortable, the mixture of odds and ends which spell the history of a cosy middle-class life*

When the CURTAIN *rises, it is raining. The room is empty. Then a tapping sound is heard and Lady Chalmont starts to descend the staircase. She is about sixty, quietly authoritative. She walks with the aid of a stick, and we suspect she may have suffered a stroke at some time. She calls out as she moves down the stairs*

Lady Chalmont Vera! (*after a pause, more sharply*) Vera!
Vera (*off, from the kitchen; impatiently*) All right—I'm coming.

As Lady Chalmont reaches the foot of the stairs, Vera emerges from the kitchen, wiping her hands on a dishcloth. She is housekeeper-companion to Lady Chalmont, and is fifty years of age

While Lady Chalmont always retains a cool, authoritative air in dealing with Vera, the housekeeper remains stubbornly, cheerfully familiar

Vera Now what?
Lady Chalmont Where's Isabel?
Vera How should I know?
Lady Chalmont It's Wednesday. She always brings me my new books on Wednesday.
Vera Perhaps she's had to work late.
Lady Chalmont It's half-day closing at the library.
Vera Well perhaps they're stock-taking or something. She'll be here. It's not that late. Stop worrying and have a cup of tea.
Lady Chalmont Yes, all right.

Lady Chalmont moves to a comfortable-looking, chintz-covered wing-chair

Vera bustles back to the kitchen. It is a swing door which allows her some effective exits and entrances, which Vera employs as though born to be an actress

Vera (*as she goes*) Of course, you never know—

Lady Chalmont's attention is engaged. She waits with a frown for Vera to return

   Vera enters, carrying a ready-set tea-tray

—it could be her boy-friend. Perhaps she's out on a date with him.
Lady Chalmont What boy-friend?
Vera Aha! (*She puts the tray by the wing-chair*)
Lady Chalmont (*impatiently*) Vera, do cut out the melodrama. You give the slightest news such a build-up. I wouldn't mind but it always turns out to be so uninteresting . . .
Vera It's Mr Michaels.
Lady Chalmont The new teacher?
Vera Yes.
Lady Chalmont What about him?
Vera (*knowingly*) She's been seen with him.
Lady Chalmont Well in a place this size, it would be difficult for her not to be seen with him, some time, somewhere. I don't see that that piece of news calls for any—(*she imitates rather well*)—aha's?

The kettle whistles from the kitchen

   Vera, offended, puts her nose up in the air and swings back into the kitchen

Lady Chalmont (*calling after Vera*) Now if it had been the Vicar . . .

   Vera swings back into the room, transformed, beaming

Vera Funny you should say that . . .
Lady Chalmont (*firmly*) Vera! I do not want to hear that ridiculous story about the Vicar and Mrs Petts.
Vera (*disappointed*) Oh. All right.

   Grumpily, Vera swings back through the door into the kitchen

After a pause the kettle whistle ceases. Lady Chalmont arranges the things on the tea-tray

   A pause then Vera comes back, carrying a teapot

Vera I know, anyway.
Lady Chalmont What?
Vera Why you're so keen to see Isabel.
Lady Chalmont Oh?
Vera (*stirring the teapot*) I saw the post this morning.
Lady Chalmont (*drily*) Taken to reading my mail now, have you?
Vera Don't need to, do I? Blue stripey airmail envelope. Funny foreign stamps.

Lady Chalmont And you know I've had a letter from my nephew John, in Dakar. It doesn't take Sherlock Holmes.

Lady Chalmont moves to pour the tea. Vera waves her away, pours—for both of them

Vera No. I'd like to have been a detective though—must be very interesting —you know, all that probing they do . . .
Lady Chalmont Yes, I'm sure you'd enjoy it.
Vera (*casually*) Any news then? (*She sits on the sofa*)
Lady Chalmont News?
Vera From John?
Lady Chalmont There is but I hate telling things twice over. So if you could possibly control your curiosity, we'll wait for Isabel.
Vera I don't mind.
Lady Chalmont Good.
Vera She's here now, anyway.
Lady Chalmont Where?
Vera She was coming up the lane while I was in the kitchen just now.
Lady Chalmont (*exasperated*) Well why couldn't you say so? Get her another cup.
Vera (*rising, offended*) I'm going to. Give us a chance.

We see Isabel in the garden, through the glass doors at the back. She smiles and waves to Lady Chalmont. She is twenty-four, charming, shy, very pretty

Lady Chalmont (*waving back*) There she is. Open the door for her.

Vera sighs heavily, moves to the picture windows at the back and slides one side open for Isabel to enter

Isabel Hello, Vera. How are you?
Vera Do this, do that. Make the tea. Open the doors. You need six pairs of hands in this place and feet to go with them . . . (*All this rendered as she closes the door after Isabel, she goes back to collect the teapot*)

Vera sweeps through into the kitchen. She returns immediately with a cup and saucer, before Isabel has had a chance to move down stage and embrace Lady Chalmont

Vera I'm fine thanks. How are you, dear? Seen that nice Mr. Michaels lately? I'll just top up the pot.

Vera disappears back into the kitchen

Isabel smiles, deposits the parcel of books she has brought, kisses Lady Chalmont on the cheek

Isabel Hello, Lady Chalmont. I'm sorry I'm late. Mind I don't make you wet. (*She takes off the rainhat and raincoat she wears*)

Lady Chalmont That's all right, my dear. It's so kind of you to come and see me. In this weather, I can't even get out into the garden. And without my books, in this house, with only Vera—(*she whispers*)—I'd go mad!

Vera returns with the teapot

Vera Whispering again?

Vera pours tea for Isabel and replenishes the other cups

We were getting quite worried about you.
Lady Chalmont Do join us for tea, Vera.
Vera I haven't got a lot of time. But just to hear the news.

Vera and Isabel sit.

Isabel What news?
Lady Chalmont (*quickly*) We hoped you might have something to tell us. You hear all the gossip in the library.
Isabel Plenty of gossip, yes. But not much real fact. (*She frowns*) People are complaining a lot about these—Hell's Angels or whatever they call themselves.
Lady Chalmont Who are they?
Vera Just a lot of hooligans in black leather jackets.
Isabel And on motor bikes. I ran into them today. That's one of the reasons I'm a bit late.
Lady Chalmont What did they do?
Vera (*excitedly*) Rape? Was it rape? It's best to tell an older woman.
Isabel I'm sorry to disappoint you. No more than childish horseplay, really. They were in the square, and suddenly started riding around me, in a circle—you know like those old American films on TV. It was silly but—frightening. They're children—but big, brutal children.
Lady Chalmont How horrid. I'd have been terrified.
Vera I'd have clumped them.
Isabel I did.
Lady Chalmont Good for you.
Isabel I just stood there, trying to get through, and I couldn't. And I knew I had to break that circle. So—without thinking almost—I just hit out with my string bag, with those rather heavy books in it—and I knocked one off his bike . . .
Lady Chalmont No!
Vera Then what happened?
Isabel Nothing really. I was petrified for a moment, expecting them all to turn on me. But they just rushed to help pick up their mate.
Lady Chalmont Was he hurt?
Isabel No. Not at all. It was the bike they were worried about. Terrified it might have got a scratch.
Vera Kids. Just big ugly kids.
Isabel And while their attention was distracted, I just ran.
Vera (*disappointed*) They didn't follow?

Act I, Scene 1 5

Isabel No. Sorry I can't make it more dramatic.
Vera We haven't had a rape around here for years.
Lady Chalmont I should hope not. Constable Tidmarsh is a very good man. I must say, wherever one goes, he's always there, on his bicycle—so much more comforting, I feel, than those Panda cars which just whizz past you.
Vera It's about time he sorted out this lot then.
Lady Chalmont He will, I am sure.
Vera He probably has trouble keeping up with them, on that old bike.
Isabel They are a bit of a menace. The chemist's shop in Moreton was broken into last weekend, while they were over there. After drugs, I suppose.
Vera And there's been robberies, three in the last month. They got into Major Buckley's house only the other night.
Lady Chalmont (*anxiously*) What, these same—angels?
Isabel We don't know that.
Vera Who else?
Isabel It might have been anyone. Robberies tend to go in series—a thief just happens to pick on a neighbourhood . . .
Lady Chalmont You are both making me quite nervous. (*She clutches her heart*) Vera, I'd better take one of my pills.
Isabel (*rising*) I'll get them for you . . .
Vera (*rising*) No, I'll get them. I keep them in the kitchen. We need some more water in the pot anyway—(*she moves to the kitchen with the teapot*) —what would anyone want to steal here?

Vera exits to the kitchen

Lady Chalmont My paintings, of course. (*She is quite disturbed at the thought*)

Vera returns, without the teapot, with a bottle of pills

Vera I can't see anything in them myself. (*She dumps down the pill box*) Pills.
Lady Chalmont (*with asperity*) Nevertheless, they are exceedingly valuable. Ask Isabel if you don't believe me.
Isabel Yes they are.
Vera (*observing the paintings critically*) Well I can't imagine anyone wanting to break in and steal them . . .
Lady Chalmont It's all right for you. You don't live in this old house all alone.
Vera (*considering*) It is a bit remote. You could scream out and nobody'd hear you.
Isabel Vera! Stop it.
Lady Chalmont I always find her such a great comfort.
Isabel You'd better take your pill.
Vera I'll get you some tea, to wash it down. (*As she swings through to the kitchen*) Wouldn't give you tuppence for them myself.

Vera exits

Isabel supervises as Lady Chalmont takes her pill

Lady Chalmont That has made up my mind. Who was it who wanted the pictures for an exhibition?
Isabel The Arts Council.
Lady Chalmont Be a darling and write to them for me. Say they can have them. They'll be insured, of course?
Isabel Oh I'm sure they will be. They're responsible for everything.
Lady Chalmont I didn't want to part with them, even for a few months. But now I'll feel much easier. With that gang of cut-throats around.

Vera enters with the teapot

Vera Have I missed anything?
Lady Chalmont (*with a sigh*) No. I don't think so.
Vera You haven't told her yet then? About the letter.
Lady Chalmont Vera, I do wish you would let *me* tell *my* news.
Isabel What letter? (*She is visibly affected*) Not from—John?
Vera Who else?
Lady Chalmont (*crossly*) Vera!
Isabel (*trying to keep her voice very calm*) Is he—coming home?

In an attempt to display calm, Isabel starts to pour more tea for them, but the spout of the pot rattles nervously against the cup. Vera takes the pot from her

Vera Here. Let me. We don't want any breakages.
Lady Chalmont You can talk. A cup and a plate last week. My best Spode.
Vera It couldn't be helped. And I stuck them together again.
Isabel Please—do tell me—what did John have to say?
Lady Chalmont (*gently*) Well—he wants to come here for a short visit— (*with kind firmness*)—with his wife.
Isabel Aurelia?
Vera Funny name, that.
Lady Chalmont (*to Isabel*) Yes.
Vera I've never known anyone called Aurelia before. Nice looking woman though, I must say.
Isabel Did he send any photographs?
Lady Chalmont No. Not this time.
Vera Bit older than him though, I'd imagine. Still, he probably needed someone like that, to put him straight . . .

Isabel has to turn away, to prevent herself sobbing. Lady Chalmont is angry with Vera

Lady Chalmont Vera! No-one asked you to drag up the past.
Vera Oh come on. If he's coming back here, it's going to be dragged up anyway. And what did I say to upset her?
Lady Chalmont You know Isabel's feelings. I'm really angry with you, Vera . . .

Act I, Scene 1

Isabel (*turning back to them*) No, please—Lady Chalmont, don't be cross with Vera—she's right, she didn't say anything . . .
Vera There you are.
Isabel (*trying to smile*) There was never anything between us, anyway. It was just—well—we were friends from childhood. He was my first—not so much, boy-friend, as hero. I loved him, I admit, but in a very childish sort of way. I admired him so much, he really was a hero to me. That's why it was all so awful when . . . (*She cannot go on. She relapses into silence, looks down at her hands*)
Lady Chalmont (*gently*) I know, my dear.
Vera (*helpfully*) Nice boy, but weak. I mean, I saw it coming . . .
Lady Chalmont Then you might have told me.
Vera How could I? Like a son to you, wasn't he! Apple of your eye. You'd never have believed me. But I knew he was in trouble, gambling and so on. Everyone knew, except you . . .
Lady Chalmont Well I found out, didn't I? When he tried to rob me. And so now that you have succeeded in digging up an unpleasant memory, perhaps you'd be kind enough to leave me to have a talk with Isabel alone.
Vera All right. If you want to be like that. (*Rising in high dudgeon*) I don't have to stay here, you know. Mrs Dolby has offered me twice as much to look after her. I just happen to be loyal, that's all. I mean, twenty years may not be much to you, but to me, it means something. But if you want to treat me like a servant, all right. I don't mind drinking my tea in the kitchen on my own. I don't mind at all.

Vera sweeps out, with her cup of tea

Isabel (*looking after Vera, biting her lip*) Oh dear, I . . .
Lady Chalmont Don't worry about it. I get this at least once a week.
Isabel But if she walks out on you . . .
Lady Chalmont She won't. No further than the kitchen. (*In a whisper*) She can hear from there.
Isabel I'm sorry. It was me being stupid that started all this . . .
Lady Chalmont Now forget it. No-one has been silly. Or perhaps we all have. Vera's quite right, of course. She usually is. We can't try and forget the past—and certainly not when it comes back to visit us.
Isabel (*eagerly*) Do let them come here, Lady Chalmont. Please try and forgive him. I know he didn't mean it.
Lady Chalmont I'm not so sure. And I don't know I can. It's not in my nature to be forgiving. That may make me mean and miserable, but that's how it is. I loved that boy, and tried to give him everything. When he became an orphan, I took the place of his parents. If he was in trouble, he could have come to me.
Isabel But he couldn't—because he loved you—he didn't want to hurt you, by knowing—he knew how you idolized him . . .
Lady Chalmont (*drily*) So he robbed me instead. Very thoughtful.
Isabel It sounds grotesque, I know. But if you hadn't caught him rifling

your desk that night—you would have thought it was a burglar—you were insured . . .

Lady Chalmont And we would have all lived happy ever after. Come on, Isabel, you're grown up now. If he had got away with that, who knows what would have come next. In a way, it was probably a good thing I did catch him red-handed. At least it was me and not the police.

Isabel (*sadly*) Yes—I suppose . . .

Lady Chalmont (*gently*) Even if it did mean him going away. He had to learn to stand on his own two feet, Isabel. There was the plantation his father had left him. Not much, but it was his own. I paid his fare out to Africa and then—well it was up to him. And if you can believe what he writes, he's grateful to me.

Isabel (*quickly*) I'm sure he is.

Lady Chalmont Forgive me for being sceptical. He implies he has been successful. Obviously, he's made enough money for him and his wife to come over here. Whether it's for a holiday or not, is not very clear. I just hope it's not to try and borrow more money.

Isabel I'm sure it's not. Oh, I do wish you'd think more kindly of him. He probably wants to make amends. And he wants to see you again. And don't tell me you don't want to see him—I just shan't believe you . . .

Lady Chalmont (*with a shrug*) I'm curious, of course . . .

Isabel Of course you are. And you must be dying to see Aurelia.

Lady Chalmont (*after a pause*) Yes. I suppose I am. Vera's right, it is a strange name. But, funny, you know it gives me a sort of shiver when I hear it. I wonder why.

Isabel Because she's John's wife, your niece, your daughter almost.

Lady Chalmont You are a funny child.

Isabel What have I said?

Lady Chalmont Nothing. But you are far more a daughter to me than Aurelia will ever be, I suspect. But we'll see.

Isabel You'll let them come then? What are their plans?

Lady Chalmont I'll give you the letter to read. They're flying to London next week, on business, and they'll telephone from there.

Isabel Next week? So soon?

Lady Chalmont Yes, well—it's these aeroplanes—they're frightfully fast. (*She rises from her chair*) You are so good, Isabel—you don't hate Aurelia at all, do you? (*She moves to the desk*)

Isabel No, of course not. Why should I?—I was so worried about John when he went out there—when he wrote and told us he was getting married, I was happy for him—it meant that he'd settled down, found himself—and she looks so beautiful in her photographs . . .

Lady Chalmont (*with a grunt*) You know what they say about beauty. (*She rummages in her bag*) Here—here's the letter—it's here somewhere. (*She finds a letter and hands it over*) I'm glad we had the chance of a little chat. To tell you the truth, I was more worried about its effect on you, than anything. I wouldn't have wanted you to stay away from here . . .

Isabel I wouldn't . . .

Lady Chalmont You did.

Act I, Scene 2

Isabel I did then, yes. I couldn't bear the thought of him not being here . . .
Lady Chalmont And you hated me.
Isabel (*after a pause*) Yes, for a time, I think I did. I couldn't see any wrong in John, ever. But—(*she forces a smile*)—it was a long time ago, wasn't it? I suppose I've grown up now. I can see things more clearly, other people's points of view.

Lady Chalmont nods, starts to move with the aid of her stick towards the kitchen

Lady Chalmont I'll leave you with the letter . . . while I go and make my peace with Vera. (*Loudly*) I do hope she'll forgive me. (*In her normal voice*) We play this scene once a week too.

Lady Chalmont smiles and hobbles into the kitchen. We hear her greet Vera and then the soft hubble-bubble of their voices off

The Lights dim slowly as Isabel reads the letter, with intensity. We see, in spite of the persuasiveness of her last speech, that she still feels a strong passion towards John. As the Lights dim to a single spot on her, Isabel holds the letter to her breast as though embracing it. She speaks, very softly, almost without voice, his name

Isabel John.

The Lights fade to a Black-out

SCENE 2

The same. About noon, four days later

The sun is shining brightly outside and the garden looks charming through the picture window. The glass door is open. In the centre of the room there is a small pile of good-quality travelling cases

As the CURTAIN *rises, Vera bustles in from the kitchen. She wears an apron and carries a vase of flowers. From above, two voices are heard, indistinctly, from the first floor. One of them is Lady Chalmont's. The other, as we will soon learn, is that of Aurelia*

Vera (*grumbling to herself*) That's right. Put the flowers in water. Fetch up the cases. What is this, a hotel? They'll be leaving their boots outside their bedroom doors next. (*She continues grumbling all the time as she sets down the flowers, picks up two of the suitcases, drags them up the stairs, imitating different voices*) Call the maid, dear. What's her name? Vera? Hello, room service? Yes, Vera here. I say, your lawn looks in good shape, what's the name of your gardener? Vera? Really?

Vera exits upstairs. A moment for pause, then Isabel appears in the garden.

She halts at the threshold immediately struck by the suitcases there. Lady Chalmont starts to descend the staircase, talking over her shoulder

Lady Chalmont But Vera, I did ask you to put the soap in the bathroom. (*Patiently, at a blurred and indistinct reply*) No. I didn't *tell* you, I *asked* you . . . (*She continues down as Isabel comes into the room, and sees her*) Isabel . . . my darling . . .

Isabel (*with a nod at the suitcases; excitedly*) They're here then?

Lady Chalmont Well yes and no. They are not here, but she is. (*She reaches the foot of the stairs and puts a consoling hand on Isabel's shoulder*) John was held up at the last moment. But he is coming.

Isabel (*bitterly disappointed*) Oh—I see . . .

There is a momentarily awkward silence broken by Vera coming down the stairs, still grumbling

Vera Put the soap in the bathroom, Vera, pop down to the village, Vera, I tell you I'm cook, housemaid, parlourmaid, kitchenmaid, butler and chauffeur. They say you can't get domestic staff these days, they're joking, ask Lady Chalmont, she's cracked it, she's got the whole lot rolled into one, until a certain someone goes across to Mrs Dolby for treble the money, anyway . . .

Vera exits into the kitchen. At the same moment Aurelia appears at the top of the stairs. She is in her thirties, beautiful with a compelling, almost hypnotic, personality. She wears a stunning costume. An elegant, feminine, mysterious lady

Aurelia Vera darling, would you fetch my white week-end case for me . . . (*She cuts off as she sees Isabel*) Oh.

Lady Chalmont Aurelia, my dear, let me introduce . . .

Aurelia cuts her off with a wave of the hand, as she descends

Aurelia No—there's no need. It's Isabel.

Aurelia, at the foot of the stairs, smiles sweetly and extends her hand

Isabel (*shyly*) Yes. (*She moves to shake hands*)

Aurelia (*warmly*) John told me so much about you. I know what good friends you were.

Lady Chalmont Isabel is an angel. I don't know what I'd do without her.

Vera carrying a bar of soap, enters from the kitchen, on the move towards the stairs

Vera I don't know what you'd do without me, but you'll find out before long, I'm telling you. (*As she passes Isabel*) Are you staying for lunch? (*Before Isabel can answer*) You might as well, I've prepared for four. (*She starts to climb the stairs*)

Act I, Scene 2

Lady Chalmont (*appealingly*) Vera . . .
Vera Yes, all right. I'm doing all I can, quick as I know how. (*She brandishes the soap*) Soap, soap, you said, remember?

Vera disappears at the top of the stairs

Lady Chalmont looks annoyed. Isabel controls a smile. Aurelia spots it and they smile together. It is a first moment of intimacy between them. Lady Chalmont limps towards her chair

Lady Chalmont I don't suppose you have staff problems in Africa.
Aurelia (*smiling sympathetically*) We do—but they're rather different ones . . .
Isabel You'll find Vera awfully sweet, really. She just takes a bit of getting used to.
Lady Chalmont That's an understatement. I can't get used to her after twenty years.
Isabel What was it you were asking for Aurelia, when you came down? The white case? Let me take it up for you.

Aurelia stops her with a smile as Isabel moves towards the case

Aurelia No, it's all right. I only wanted it for your presents. I can give them to you here. (*She takes up the white case and opens it*) They're from John.

(*She hands a package to Lady Chalmont*)

Lady Chalmont (*feeling the rather bulky package curiously*) I wonder what it is.
Aurelia And there's one for you. (*She hands a package to Isabel*)
Isabel For me? From John?
Aurelia (*without any edge*) From both of us.
Isabel Thank you.

Isabel starts to open her smaller package while Lady Chalmont still tries to figure out what is inside her own parcel

Lady Chalmont What on earth is it?

Isabel gasps with pleasure as she opens the package and takes out of the box inside a necklace of coloured stones

Isabel Oh, it's lovely.
Aurelia They're moonstones. They're supposed to bring good luck.
Lady Chalmont Well—let's see what I've got. (*She starts to peel off the wrappers*)

Isabel moves to a mirror on one of the side walls, holds the necklace up to her throat so that she can see the effect. Aurelia smiles, moves with her

Aurelia It looks lovely on you. Here, let me fix it . . .

Isabel smiles thanks at her. Plainly, a relationship has been struck up quickly between the two women

Aurelia There—now that is really beautiful.
Lady Chalmont (*almost at the end of her task, glancing across*) Lovely . . . (*As she finishes unwrapping*) Oh, how hideous!

Lady Chalmont is appalled at the ghastly looking African mask which is her present. Isabel, seeing it, controls a giggle. Again there is an exchange of intimate glances between her and Aurelia, as Aurelia asks, with straight-faced sincerity:

Aurelia Don't you like it?
Lady Chalmont (*trying to be polite*) Er—yes—when I say it is hideous, I mean, er, the whole point of this type of mask was just that, to be hideous, frighten off vengeful gods and so on . . .

Aurelia and Isabel continue to conceal their amusement at her discomfiture

   Vera starts to descend the staircase, muttering to herself

Vera Soap's in the bathroom, I've put out the clean towels, changed all the sheets, Hoovered the edges . . .
Lady Chalmont (*simultaneously*) Good, lets all have a glass of sherry then . . .
Vera (*without looking at them, as she crosses to the kitchen*) Pour the sherry, Vera, put out some crisps . . .
Lady Chalmont (*crossly*) Vera!

Vera stops, turns, is terribly formal

Vera Yes, my lady?
Lady Chalmont I was going to ask you if you would join us in a glass of sherry? I'm sure Isabel won't mind pouring for us.
Isabel No, of course not.
Vera (*thawing immediately*) Oh, well . . .
Isabel But do let me show you my present first—from John and Aurelia—isn't it lovely?

Vera comes over to join the group, standing near Lady Chalmont's chair

Vera Yes—very nice . . .
Lady Chalmont And what about mine? (*She turns in her chair to Vera, suddenly holding up the mask to her face*) Eh?
Vera Aaaah! (*She clutches at her breast as the others all laugh*) God—you scared the daylights out of me—how'd you like to meet that in the dark?
Lady Chalmont It would give me a heart attack, I'm sure.

Isabel moves away to pour the drinks

Vera And that reminds me. Only one sherry for you. You know what the doctor said.
Lady Chalmont Vera, don't nag. I'm a strong old bird really. And I lead a quiet life. We don't get a lot of excitement, do we?

Isabel hands round the drinks on a tray

Vera Excitement? No, never. (*She sips at her drink, considers*) Unless you believe what they say about the Vicar.

Act I, Scene 2

Lady Chalmont Well I don't. The village makes up these stories because it's so bored.
Aurelia Is it really just a village here, then?
Vera There's not much to do. The big event of the year is the pantomime at the Church Hall.
Isabel You'll find it all very different.
Aurelia Not really. Ours is a big country. But a small community.
Lady Chalmont But do you like it?
Aurelia I was born there. It's my home.
Lady Chalmont And John?
Aurelia (*with a shrug*) He has done well, made a success of the plantation. But I think his heart is in England.
Vera (*pouring herself another drink*) There'll always be an England.
Lady Chalmont Vera, mind how you go with that sherry. Remember what happened when you cooked the Christmas pudding.
Vera (*defensively*) I was only tasting the ingredients. And sherry and brandy don't mix, not in my stomach anyway. And I do have a bit of a light head for drink, I must confess. Not like John. (*She laughs heartily*) He could really knock it back.

Vera continues laughing until she suddenly realizes she is the only one

Lady Chalmont (*quietly*) I thought we weren't going back over the past history?
Vera Now what have I said?
Aurelia (*quickly*) Out there, everyone drinks. It is a social crime not to. (*A tiny pause*) John drinks no more than anyone else—and no less.
Vera Got held up on business, did he?
Aurelia Yes. A neighbour is selling his estate. And that's a rather complicated business these days. John stayed to help. It should only take a few days.
Isabel What's it like, your life there?
Aurelia Oh—a bit boring. John's away all day. There's not a lot for me to do.
Lady Chalmont But doesn't he work on the plantation, where you live?
Aurelia Oh yes, but it is awfully big. I don't see him until the evening.
Lady Chalmont You have friends you can visit?
Aurelia Yes. But everything is so distant there. One might drive two hundred miles just to go to a party. And in the rainy season, we are just stuck, literally. The whole place becomes a bog.
Vera We get quite a lot of rain here.
Aurelia (*smiling*) Believe me, you have never seen rain. I sometimes feel I am living in an aquarium. In one day, we would get your rainfall for a year.
Vera Of course we get snow, too. You don't.
Aurelia (*exchanging a quick smiling glance with Isabel*) No, I must say, snow has never been a problem. (*With sudden enthusiasm*) But you know what you have here? Culture. Theatres, museums, the opera, the ballet. This is what I'd like to see while I'm here.
Lady Chalmont You must get some time off, Isabel. Show Aurelia around.
Aurelia I'd like that. But you'll join us, Aunt Margaret, won't you?

Lady Chalmont I'd like to. I'd love to get to London. Or even Oxford. But it's no use. My leg is too painful. And Doctor Redford doesn't like me travelling far.
Aurelia Then we'll go and see everything for you, tell you all about it. Will you really be able to get time off, Isabel?
Isabel Yes, I think so. We have a system of time-saving at the library. I've got the best part of a week due to me, and that's without the holidays.
Lady Chalmont There you are then, that's settled.
Aurelia I'll hire a car. That way, I'll see the countryside.
Lady Chalmont Good idea.
Aurelia We'll have great fun, I know we will.
Vera (*a little drunk on her two sherries*) It'll give the village something to talk about.
Lady Chalmont (*crossly*) What on earth has it got to do with the village?
Vera Well—they know how Isabel felt about John—they're expecting her and Aurelia to be at daggers drawn.
Isabel (*with uncharacteristic coldness*) It just goes to show how wrong the village can be, doesn't it?
Lady Chalmont Or those half a dozen gossiping biddies that Vera likes to think makes up the village.
Aurelia Yes—please tell them, Vera, from me, that we are good friends. Very good friends.

Vera suddenly realizes that everyone is against her and goes on the defensive

Vera Well don't look at me. I never indulge in gossip myself. But you can't help overhearing . . . and I'm just telling you what people will say.

The telephone rings

Vera I'll get it . . . (*She takes a pace or two, staggers slightly, holds on to a table*)
Lady Chalmont Let Isabel go.

Isabel moves to the desk

Vera What for?
Lady Chalmont Because she can walk in a straight line. It's quicker.

Aurelia takes a cigarette and lighter from the sofa table. Vera remains holding on to her table

Isabel Hello? (*She answers the phone*) Yes? Oh, just a moment please. (*She cups the phone, nods to Aurelia*) It's for you.

Aurelia, about to light her cigarette, drops it, taken aback

Aurelia For me? But no-one knows I'm here.
Lady Chalmont Perhaps it's John? (*She looks at Isabel*)
Isabel No. I know John's voice. And anyway, it's a call box. (*She gestures silence to the others. Into the phone*) Who is it calling please? Just a moment. (*She cups the phone again*) A Mr Mercer. (*As Aurelia hesitates*) Do you want me to say you're out?

Act I, Scene 2 15

Aurelia (*moving to the phone*) No. It doesn't matter. (*She forces a smile for Isabel as she takes the phone from her*) Hello? . . . Yes, that's right. I'm fine, how are you? (*She listens*) No, John is still out there. I'm waiting to hear definitely when he is coming. (*She listens, hesitates*) No, I—well thank you for the invitation but I really am rather tied up—yes, my aunt, and I have a friend here. I really wouldn't be able to manage it. (*She controls, not too successfully, a fairly obvious unease*) Yes, perhaps when John arrives . . . Yes, do call again . . . no, I'm sorry . . . all right, goodbye . . . (*She puts down the phone, shrugs, forces a smile*) It's a character who was on the same plane coming over here. He's got an important agency out there. I don't like him very much—but he goes to the same club as John—and out there, that makes him some kind of bloodbrother . . .
Lady Chalmont Yes—I know the type. Vera, I hope you don't mind my mentioning the subject, but you haven't forgotten lunch, have you?

Vera is still at the table where she halted en route for the phone

Vera (*with a gasp*) The duck!

During the following, Isabel looks at Aurelia, concerned at her unease during the telephone conversation

Lady Chalmont Yes.
Vera It's in the oven.
Lady Chalmont Exactly my point.
Vera I must go.
Lady Chalmont I think you should.

Vera pursues a reasonably straight line towards the kitchen

Vera (*excitedly, as she exits*) I never should be forced to drink sherry.

Vera exits to the kitchen, swinging through the door

Lady Chalmont (*shaking her head*) There—you've well and truly met our treasure Vera.
Aurelia I think she is very amusing. (*She is aware that Isabel is looking at her*) Now—what was it we were talking about? Oh, yes, our trip to London. Do you know, there are three cities I have always longed to visit. Paris, which I saw when the plane landed there yesterday. London, which you are going to take me to see, I hope. And New York, which maybe I will see some time.

Vera comes out of the kitchen and marches towards the centre of the room

Vera Everything's all right, all in order, lunch will be in twenty minutes. (*She starts back towards the kitchen*)

The front doorbell rings

O.K., I'll get it.

Lady Chalmont Isabel, is she fit to answer the front door?

Vera exits through the kitchen

Isabel It's too late to stop her.

The sound of Vera's voice, the door closing, then she comes marching back into the room

Vera Overseas telegram.
Lady Chalmont For me?
Vera No. (*She hands the telegram form to Aurelia, starts back*) Don't forget, twenty minutes.

Vera exits

Isabel (*as Aurelia opens the telegram*) Is it from John?
Aurelia I expect so. (*She reads*) Yes. Damn. (*To Lady Chalmont*) Sorry. (*She reads*) "Apologize delay may be ten days will cable again love to all John."
Lady Chalmont Oh dear. (*Consolingly*) Well—it'll give you some time to see England. (*To Isabel*) You might as well claim that week off, my dear. Pour Aurelia another drink. And have one yourself.
Isabel (*moving to the drinks tray*) Won't you?
Lady Chalmont No. Better not. It really does affect me. Even that one. In fact, I think I'd better lie down till lunch, just in case.
Aurelia (*moving to Lady Chalmont*) Aunt Margaret, you should have said if you didn't feel well.
Lady Chalmont I'm fine, really. Just being cautious.
Isabel Let me help you up to your room.
Lady Chalmont Thank you.

The telephone rings

Don't let Vera answer it.
Isabel (*moving to the phone*) All right.
Aurelia I'll see Lady Chalmont upstairs.

Aurelia assists Lady Chalmont up the stairs as Isabel answers the phone

Isabel (*on the phone*) Hello?... Yes. All right, I'll take it down. Who is it for?... Yes... (*She scribbles on a pad*) Yes, I've got that... (*She listens, writes*) Yes. Is that all?... Well thank you for telephoning but we have already received that telegram. Yes—(*quickly*)—just a minute... (*She glances upstairs*)

Aurelia and Lady Chalmont have disappeared from view

Did you say that was sent from Paris?... Yesterday?... Are you sure?... (*A pause*) No, nothing's wrong. Perfectly all right. Just a mix-up... Yes, we have received the telegram. Thank you.

Act I, Scene 3

The Lights dim rapidly as Isabel replaces the phone, a single spot illuminating Isabel as she looks up the stairs after Aurelia. Then this fades to a Black-out

Scene 3

The same. Night, four days later

Bright moonlight is shining on the garden, through the picture window. After a moment there is the sound of a car halting, engine cutting out, doors slamming. Then muffled laughter is heard from Aurelia and Isabel. They enter through the kitchen, stifling their giggles and "shushing" each other as they turn on various lights. Both have on evening dresses, with cloaks over them. Isabel twirls round in a dance, while Aurelia unfastens the cloak she wears

Aurelia Oh, lovely. I haven't had so many laughs in years. I felt like twenty-five again.

Isabel You don't even look twenty-five.

Aurelia Bless you for that. (*She moves to Isabel, caresses her cheek gently*) Bless you for everything. You've made my stay so happy.

Isabel I feel—(*struggling with her embarrassment*)—almost as though I'd never lived—until you came here. (*With sudden fear*) I can't bear to think of you going...

Aurelia embraces her, comforts her, then smiles, moves away

Aurelia Let's worry about that when it happens, shall we? (*Lightheartedly*) I might even persuade John to stay here.

Isabel (*delighted*) Really? Would you really?

Aurelia Why not? I love evenings like this. Early dinner, a show...

Isabel Which we hated.

Aurelia So we left. That's what was so delightful. No-one minded when we missed the second half. No-one cared. We were free.

Aurelia laughs. So does Isabel

Isabel (*giggling*) I don't know what we're laughing about. It was a terrible evening really. We should never have gone on to that discotheque.

Aurelia Oh, I don't know. I met that handsome man. The one four foot eleven tall with the funny walk and the high voice.

Isabel You can't have everything.

Aurelia True. At least he didn't have B.O. like the big, butch blond boy.

Isabel You can't win them all.

Aurelia (*moving to her*) You were all right. There were plenty of handsome young men buzzing around you.

Isabel They were boring. It was more fun being with you.

Aurelia looks at her. They are close together

Aurelia Was it?

You looked very happy, and so beautiful.
Isabel If I did, it was these beautiful clothes you gave me. (*She pirouettes, swirling the cloak*) Oh, I love this cloak. (*She hugs it to her*) I feel I don't want to take it off, ever.
Aurelia Yes. Take it off. Let me see you in that gown.

Aurelia reaches forward to unclasp the cloak. Isabel makes no attempt to stop her. Aurelia lets the cloak trail. Isabel, in a beautifully styled, rather daringly low-cut dress, returns her glance evenly. The two women look at each other for a moment

Aurelia (*after a pause*) I shall miss you.

Isabel quickly embraces her

Isabel Oh, don't. Let's not even think about it.

Aurelia embraces her in return, kisses her on the cheek. Isabel breaks away, smiling

I know, let's raid the sideboard, have a drink.
Aurelia Not that awful sherry, please.
Isabel Plum wine?

Aurelia makes a face

I know—there's some brandy—kept for strictly medicinal purposes, of course.
Aurelia I do feel a little faint.
Isabel (*taking a brandy bottle from the sideboard*) Me too. (*She pours*) You and I will be right old drunkards before long. (*Considering*) I shouldn't have said that, should I?

Aurelia sits. Isabel brings the drinks across and sits opposite her

Aurelia Why not? Because of John? He's not that bad.
Isabel (*leaning forward*) Tell me.

Aurelia raises an enquiring eyebrow

All about it. How you met him.
Aurelia (*smiling*) Oh. That. Well—it was about a year after he left here, I suppose—nowhere particularly romantic—it was at a friend's cocktail party—all rather boring business people—they used to make me want to scream sometimes—and my husband was the most boring of them all...
Isabel (*surprised*) Your—?
Aurelia Oh, didn't John say? Yes, I was married before—to a middle-aged, middle-class jeweller. He was twenty years older than John and—oh, John had just come out from England—he was so new, so refreshing—I don't know exactly what it was—it happened so quickly for both of us, we just—let it happen—we didn't try to analyse it. (*She sighs*) Anyway, we ran away—there was a bit of a scandal, but not for long, only until the next marriage in that set broke up, when they had something else to gossip about—and by then we were married and semi-

respectable again—although it was never quite the same—we always remained—outsiders, I suppose.
Isabel But you were together.
Aurelia (*reflectively*) Yes. Too much, sometimes. When times are hard—and they were for a long time—when you're both under pressure—you can get on each other's nerves. (*She drinks*) Oh come on, that's all past—let's talk about the future.
Isabel What future?
Aurelia Tomorrow night. Where shall we go? Back to that disco again? Do you think Toulouse-Lautrec will still be there? You must admit, he gives a girl a feeling of superiority . . .

They start to giggle again and instantly shush each other

Isabel We mustn't wake Lady Chalmont.
Aurelia Is she a light sleeper?
Isabel I'm not sure. She says she is. She says the pain in her leg keeps her awake.
Aurelia How ill is she, really?
Isabel I don't know. I think she puts it on a bit. She can be quite dramatic. But it's quite true she did have a stroke. I would say that she is in bad health, and she takes good advantage of it.
Aurelia You've never really forgiven her, have you? For what she did to John?
Isabel (*shaking her head*) At the time, I could have killed her. I really could. And I've never felt that about anybody. And yet she's always been so kind to me, and I've always liked her, I really have . . .

Isabel breaks off, unable for a moment to continue. Aurelia prompts her

Aurelia But you loved John. That was the difference.
Isabel It just seemed so cruel. He was at the end of his tether. I knew it. I could sense it. But I couldn't help him. I didn't know how. But I did know he needed help—he needed forgiveness—what she did, shattered him.
Aurelia Sometimes you need breaking down—before you can build up.
Isabel Yes. I see that now. And I suppose it all worked out in the end. Well it did. John's been lucky. He's got you. But you asked me how I felt at the time, and I told you. It was—the worst moment of my life, I think . . .
Aurelia (*with a sudden smile*) It must be this brandy—we're getting so morbid.
Isabel I'm sorry, it's my fault. (*She sips, giggles*) Lovely brandy though.
Aurelia No, my fault. For asking too many questions. Let's have another.

Aurelia finishes her glass and rises to refill it. Isabel gestures to her

Isabel Better not.
Aurelia Oh, come on. Have one more, just for the road.
Isabel What road? I only live across the way.
Aurelia Well you don't have to be in at any special time, do you? And I'm enjoying myself. Just being with you. So stay a little longer. Please.

Isabel (*relenting easily*) All right. Just one more.
Aurelia I must go up to the bathroom first.
Aurelia makes for the staircase. Isabel calls out after her
Isabel Mind how you go. There's a creaky floorboard just outside Vera's room.
Aurelia stops at the foot of the staircase, turns
Aurelia Is she sleeping here tonight?
Isabel You can never tell with Vera. She has her own room but she's very temperamental. If anyone's upset her, she'll go and stay with her brother, who lives in the next village. And then, when he upsets her, or his wife, or her niece or nephew, she'll come back here to stay.
Aurelia Oh . . . (*She starts to ascend the stairs*)
Isabel But just in case, go quietly.
Aurelia Quietly.

Aurelia waves acknowledgement, then promptly stumbles, mid-way up the stairs. They shush each other, then stifle their giggles

Aurelia continues up the stairs, out of sight.

Isabel finishes her drink, goes to the sideboard

Lady Chalmont appears on the stairs, in her dressing gown. She leans over the side-rail, looks down at Isabel, first glancing over her shoulder towards where Aurelia went

Lady Chalmont Well—you're living it up, aren't you?
Isabel Oh—hello—I hope we didn't wake you.
Lady Chalmont I couldn't sleep anyway. My leg. (*She starts to move down the stairs*) Have a good evening?
Isabel The theatre was awful. We left. Went to a funny disco.
Lady Chalmont Dancing? I'm not sure John would approve.
Isabel (*taken aback*) It was only a sort of joke place.
Lady Chalmont (*at the foot of the stairs*) I'm not sure I approve. (*Before Isabel can reply*) Listen, Isabel. And don't interrupt because I want to talk to you for a few minutes, alone. And for the week, almost, you've been constantly in Aurelia's company.
Isabel But you asked me to look after her. You said . . .
Lady Chalmont I know what I said. And I know what I'm saying now. Believe me, Isabel, there's something evil about that woman.
Isabel Oh, that's ridiculous.
Lady Chalmont I know you think me just a vindictive old woman. But it's not true. John was my own flesh and blood. I always wanted to believe in him. Desperately. But inside, I always knew he was weak and foolish.
Isabel He seems to have succeeded away from here.
Lady Chalmont We only have her word for that.
Isabel John will be here soon enough. You'll be able to see for yourself.

Act I, Scene 3

Lady Chalmont I don't think he's coming. I believe they've split up. She was married before, you know. Did she tell you that?
Isabel Yes. As a matter of fact, she did.
Lady Chalmont I can't understand why John keeps putting off his trip. And who is this Mr Mercer who keeps ringing Aurelia?
Isabel She explained about him. Why are you so suspicious of everything she does?
Lady Chalmont I don't know why. But my instinct has served me well all my life. And because I care for you, I want to warn you.
Isabel It's fairly obvious to me, Lady Chalmont, that those lurid novels you insist I fetch you from the library are beginning to play on your mind. Perhaps it would be better If I didn't come here?
Lady Chalmont You know that's not what I meant... (*She breaks off as she becomes aware of Aurelia coming down the stairs*)

Aurelia enters

Aurelia Hello, Aunt Margaret. I'm sorry. Did we wake you? (*She reaches the bottom of the stairs*)
Lady Chalmont No. I was reading. I just came down to get a cup of chocolate.

Lady Chalmont starts to move towards the kitchen. Aurelia crosses to stop her

Aurelia I'll make it for you.
Lady Chalmont I don't think I want to sit up. I'm tired suddenly

Lady Chalmont turns back towards the stairs. She looks at Isabel, who refuses to meet her glance

Aurelia All right, then I'll bring it up to you.
Lady Chalmont You're very kind, but . . .
Aurelia (*insistently*) It's no trouble.
Lady Chalmont (*with a sigh, not wanting to argue*) All right. Thank you. (*As she goes up the stairs*) Good night, Isabel.

Aurelia glances quickly at them both, sensing something is wrong, then goes into the kitchen. Lady Chalmont continues sadly on her way upstairs, and exits

Isabel (*without looking at her*) Good night.

Isabel stands, stony faced, until the sound of her dragging footsteps has ceased. Then she moves, finishes her drink, picks up her cloak and fastens it around her

Aurelia comes out of the kitchen with a tray on which stands a jug of chocolate and cups.

Aurelia You're not going?
Isabel Yes.

Aurelia Did she upset you?
Isabel No.
Aurelia You're not a very good liar. (*She deposits the tray, moves close to Isabel*) Was she saying things about me?
Isabel (*hesitantly*) Yes.
Aurelia She's jealous, that's all. Of me. Of you. And now both of us. But there's no point in getting upset about it.
Isabel You're right. It was silly. I'll apologize to her tomorrow.
Aurelia Do it now. Take her chocolate up. She'd rather have it from you than me, anyway. And just say goodnight, nicely. And then we'll all sleep better.
Isabel Do you want me to?
Aurelia Yes.
Isabel Then I will.

Isabel pours chocolate from the jug into one of the cups. Aurelia goes to her bag, takes out a pill box. She gives Isabel a couple

Aurelia Here. Sleeping pills. If her leg is paining her.
Isabel You're always so thoughtful.

Aurelia smiles, but suddenly loses the smile at the sound of a car's hooter outside. She turns away from Isabel

I wonder who that is. Must be someone in the lane.
Aurelia (*without turning, finding some business to keep her away from Isabel*) A courting couple, I expect. Brushed against the horn by mistake. You'd better take that up before it's cold.

Isabel frowns, realizing that Aurelia is suddenly nervous about something

Isabel Yes. I'm going now.

Isabel goes quickly up the staircase

As soon as she is alone, Aurelia moves quickly upstage and looks out of the garden window. She sees nothing, and turns back into the room, gnawing at her knuckles anxiously

Suddenly, behind Aurelia, a man appears. This is Mercer. He is thirty-five, a smooth rogue, casually but expensively dressed, chirpy in manner, a character who lives off his wits

Aurelia does not see Mercer at first, and he is content not to let her see him. Then she half turns, and gasps at the shock of seeing him so close to her, although they are separated by the window. She waves him away. He shakes his head and points to her insistently. She takes a quick look upstairs, then opens the glass doors to let him in

Mercer Evening.
Aurelia What do you want?
Mercer What do you think?

Act I, Scene 3

Aurelia I can't talk to you now. Not here.
Mercer You'll have to, darling. I'm fed up with chasing you on the blower.
Aurelia I'm sorry. Things have been difficult. But I will meet you, I promise.
Mercer Good. When? Tomorrow?
Aurelia If you like.
Mercer I like any time. So long as you've got the money.
Aurelia You'll have to give me more time.
Mercer I've given you time already. And time's expensive. Now I warn you, I'm not going to be messed about much longer . . .
Aurelia (*in a fierce whisper*) All right! I'll get the money for you. We'll work out some way. But I can't talk about it now. I'm not alone. There's someone here with me and she'll be down at any moment.
Mercer Who's that? That rather gorgeous kid you've been carting about with you? I think I'll wait and be introduced. I rather fancy her.
Aurelia You keep your hands off that girl or, I'm warning you, I'll kill you.
Mercer (*surprised at her ferocity*) I do believe you would. All right. We won't complicate the issue. Just call me tomorrow at the local pub. That's where I'm staying. And we'll fix up how I'm going to get paid. But remember, that's all we're talking about. I don't want any more excuses. If you can't get it yourself, get it from the old lady. She must be loaded. These paintings are worth a few bob, I can tell you. (*He suddenly, surprisingly, begins to laugh*) Ha, ha, yes. Dear old Johnny. We had some nights in the club, didn't we? Those were the days. (*He looks towards the stairs*) Oh, good evening.

Isabel appears on the stairs and comes down

Aurelia swings round in the middle of his speech and realizes immediately that it has been put on for Isabel's benefit. Isabel pauses at the foot of the stairs, staring at Mercer quite coldly

Aurelia Oh—Isabel—this is Mr Mercer—I think I told you about him—he's visiting here too.
Mercer That's right. I commute, actually. It's just like taking the train to town every day, only it's a plane to another country, every week. That's the way business is today. Fast. And you've got to keep pace with it. Just like life today. Takes some keeping up with, doesn't it? Eh?

He chuckles at his intended witticism. Both women regard him stonily

Yes—well—I was just popping by—thought I'd look in, see if Johnny had arrived. I didn't ring the bell in case I woke anybody—then saw lovely here through the window . . . (*He backs to the window as he explains. Even he is put out by his stony reception*) Nice seeing you, anyway. Good night, Miss—er—Isabel. Enjoyed our chat. I'll see you then, Aurelia. Don't worry to show me out. I'll find my way. Make sure you lock up after me. You never know who's about. Yes—well . . .

And Mercer goes, being swallowed up by the night quickly as soon as he moves out of the light pool thrown by the porch-lamp outside the windows.

Aurelia, embarrassed, not knowing what Isabel has heard, does not look at her. She moves to light a cigarette for herself at the sofa table. Isabel watches her

Aurelia I'm sorry . . .
Isabel For what?
Aurelia He's an unpleasant character—as you probably sensed. I wouldn't have let him in but—well, I didn't want him making a row.
Isabel You don't have to apologize to me. It's not my house. And anyway, I'm sorry . . .

Aurelia frowns, turns to face her

Aurelia You?
Isabel I'm sorry you don't trust me.

Aurelia bites her lip, turns away again, not certain what Isabel has heard of the Mercer conversation

Aurelia I'm tired. I think I'll take some sleeping pills and turn in.
Isabel What about our chocolate?

Aurelia hesitates, shrugs, then moves towards the chocolate pot, pours two cups. She takes the pill box out of her bag, empties two pills on to the palm of her hand. She is about to take them

Isabel Aurelia . . .

Aurelia looks at her

Don't.

Aurelia frowns puzzlement

We were going to have a last brandy and a chat, weren't we? Before all these interruptions.
Aurelia I don't think brandy goes with chocolate.
Isabel Let's find out, shall we?

Aurelia shrugs reluctant assent. Isabel pours brandy for them both. It is evident now (indeed from the moment that she came down the steps) that this is a new relationship. Isabel is so much more dominant now, Aurelia so hesitant and weak. It is almost a complete reversal of their previous roles

(*Handing Aurelia her glass*) Why won't you tell me?

Aurelia watches warily as Isabel removes her cloak again and takes a chair

Aurelia What?
Isabel You're in some sort of trouble, aren't you? Perhaps I can help?
Aurelia You mean Mercer? Oh, take no notice of him. He's just a creep. Always trying to borrow money. He claims John borrowed from him.
Isabel He's very persistent, isn't he? For someone who just wants a debt repaid? (*When Aurelia does not reply*) I've seen him before you know.
Aurelia When?
Isabel At Chichester, when we went to the theatre. I saw him speak to you when I went to the powder room in the interval. And he was on the train, when we went to London. He's been following us . . .

Act I, Scene 3

Aurelia (*with difficulty*) That's typical of him—he tries to get on your nerves—so he follows you about—keeps telephoning . . .
Isabel You must know how to get rid of pests like that. But you let him go on. I know you're in trouble, Aurelia. Or Johnny is, which is more likely . . .
Aurelia Isabel—please—I'd rather not talk about it . . .
Isabel (*after a pause*) All right. Let's talk about something else.

Isabel gets up, goes across to the cabinet, looks in it, takes a photo album out of it. She brings it across to Aurelia, sits on the sofa, motions Aurelia to join her. Aurelia does as she is bid

Isabel Has this been sprung on you yet? It's Lady Chalmont's family album. There are a few shots here that might interest you. Look, there's John—he was only a little boy then—that was taken before his parents died—there's one of him at school—doesn't he look sweet? That's in the garden here, when he first arrived—he looks a little orphan, doesn't he? So lost.

Aurelia starts to weep. Isabel glances at her, then continues to turn the pages

I know there is something wrong between you and John, Aurelia. You might as well tell me. Oh, look, at school again, in the first eleven—doesn't he look proud? That's a picnic at the lake. I remember that. It must have been quite soon after I first met him. I was already in love with him, I remember that. That's a good one. Head and shoulders. You can see the expression in his eyes. He always had a little boy, orphan lost, look, didn't he? I suspect even before he became an orphan. Oh we've jumped a bit now. That's early days at Cambridge. My word, doesn't he look proud, and full of himself.

Aurelia continues to weep

What is it, Aurelia? Have you split up? You might as well tell me. If you don't he will when he comes.

Aurelia's weeping now becomes louder, uncontrolled. Isabel puts down the book and leans across to embrace her, comfort her

There, there. Hush now. I'm sorry I upset you. I only showed you the pictures because I want to help you. I don't only love John, Aurelia. I love you as well. You'll see. When he comes. I really do love you. I'm not jealous of you.
Aurelia (*through her tears*) He won't come. He won't ever come.
Isabel Because you've parted?
Aurelia (*fiercely*) Because he's dead. And I killed him!
Isabel (*recoiling with horror*) Oh . . .
Aurelia You couldn't rest until you pried my secret from me, could you? Well that's it. Your hero, John, was a monster so far as I'm concerned. He tried to kill me—*really*—he didn't just knock me about, I was used enough to that—but that night he was berserk. He *would* have killed me. But I killed him.

Isabel (*shaken*) How? Why?
Aurelia (*wearily*) Wouldn't you rather just call the police?
Isabel Aurelia! For God's sake. Tell me.
Aurelia All right. I'll tell you. But you'll have to get rid of all your illusions. And don't blame me if you're disappointed. (*She looks downstage, out at space*) He was a drunkard. You knew that. But he was twice as bad when he got out there. I fell into the classic trap. I thought I would save him from himself. Some joke. He was doing well enough at the plantation, not for what he did but because he had a good manager and trading conditions were favourable; but he drank or gambled it all away. I had to go out to work myself. A hostess in a club, would you believe it? Taking money from drunken fools like my husband to keep a drunken fool who was my husband. What a waste of time! Oh, he was all right when he was sober, those few moments of clarity like the commercials before the programme continues. Then he was the little boy lost, sweet, charming John, the one we all fell in love with and wanted to cuddle and spoil. But it didn't last.

Isabel reaches out to touch Aurelia, in compassion. Aurelia does not look at her, but takes her hand, in comfort. She continues her story, forcing herself to remember

When it happened—he was already a near alcholic—he'd been away for days on a bender of some sort—nothing unusual about that—but he usually just came back and collapsed. This time, he still had some life left in him. He wanted money. I refused. I had none, anyway. He got angry, started calling me names. I retaliated. I was mad with fury at him. Then he hit at me with a bottle. I ducked, I remember, and the bottle smashed. He looked at it, those jagged edges, and then he slashed at my face. I grabbed the first thing which came to hand. It was an old African sword, used for cutting grass. I only hit him with it once. That was enough. I'd cut an artery. I tried to put a tourniquet on him, but it was too late. Within minutes, he was dead. I panicked. There was only one thought in my mind. No sorrow, for him or me. No compassion. No hate, no love. Just survival. That was the only message my brain was pumping to me. Survive. (*She passes a hand over her eyes, exhausted at the recountal. Then goes on*) It was raining, of course. Always, out there, at the bad times, it seemed to rain. And on the plantation not far from the house, there was a patch of quicksand. I pulled John's body across the ground, then rolled him down the slope. And the quicksand just—(*her eyes recall every moment*)—slowly—swallowed—him—up.

Isabel is horrified. Aurelia takes a deep breath

The rest, you more or less know. I thought of the trip, to explain John's absence. Out there, I was always going to follow him. Over here, he was always going to follow me. Obviously, I couldn't keep it up for ever. But I was only living from day to day. That's the way I have lived, ever since. And do you know, it's better? I've had more good days, this last few weeks, than I've had I think, in my whole life. And I met you, Isabel.

Act I, Scene 3 27

I know you'll hate me now but I just want you to know, that meeting you meant more to me than anything. And I'm glad it was I who married John, and not you. Because you couldn't have taken the strain. You would have killed yourself. (*She takes a deep breath, rises*) All right—let's call the police and get it over with.
Isabel I'm not going to call the police. I want to get you out of this mess, if that's possible.
Aurelia (*surprised*) But John?
Isabel My John? He died long ago. Do you know, my mind was blanking out at some points in your story, refusing to believe what you said, because none of it conformed to my image of him. But it was an image, not a reality. You had to live with the real thing, and it was the real thing, the monstrous thing in him, which you killed. Not the John I knew. He was the look in a little boy's eyes. And that is, for me, how he'll stay. But let's worry about you...
Aurelia It's too late for that. I didn't tell you about Mercer.
Isabel You didn't have to. I overheard your conversation. All of it. Lady Chalmont was already asleep when I went up. She must have been exhausted. Anyway, I started to bring the chocolate down. And then I heard voices. I don't know why I deliberately listened, but I did. He knows, doesn't he? He's blackmailing you?
Aurelia Yes. It was sheer bad luck. That night, in Dakar, he was on his way back to town when his car started playing him up, so he thought he'd play safe and spend the night with us. That was his story, anyway. It doesn't matter why he came. He did. And he saw me. For a few days, he let it go. And then he came and saw me. I just collapsed, I admit it. I gave him every sou I could scrape together. But it wasn't enough for him. He's determined to bleed me, and there's nothing I can do about it. I've got to pay him, if I want to stay out of prison, anyway.
Isabel But where will you get the money from?
Aurelia That's the problem. I'll sell up everything, but it won't realize much. The plantation was mortgaged over and over again, down to the last bamboo.
Isabel I have some money saved. Only a few hundreds. But it's yours if it's of any help.
Aurelia It's sweet of you—I can't tell you how touched I am—especially—well, you know—but he's after thousands, not hundreds.
Isabel Well we can at least talk to him.
Aurelia (*surprised*) We?
Isabel Yes. Why not? It might help. Since he's intent on exposing you, let him see that one person at least knows what you've done and cannot condemn you. After all, it was self-defence, not murder. A jury might not even send you to prison.
Aurelia If they believed me. But not everyone's like you.
Isabel Well let's call Mercer anyway. We'll make him a straight offer, to take it or leave it. It's your only chance.
Aurelia I'll try anything to get out of this mess. When?
Isabel Now. (*She moves resolutely to the phone, starts to dial*)

Aurelia But...

Isabel The pub where he said he's staying is only down the road. He can be back here in a few minutes. Let's get it done while Lady Chalmont's fast asleep and Vera's out of the way. If you meet him anywhere else, you'll start tongues wagging. At least, this house is out of the way. There are no neighbours to pry. (*On the phone as someone answers*) Hello? Oh, Mr Mercer please... Thank you. (*A pause*) Mr Mercer? This is Isabel Reading... Yes, that's right... (*Coldly, in answer to something he says*) I don't think that's very funny... Yes, I am ringing for Aurelia. She wants to see you... Yes, now. Here... You'll come right away. (*She shudders her dislike of Mercer to Aurelia*) I don't think that's very funny either... Yes, all right, we'll see you soon. Good-bye.

As Isabel puts down the phone, both women are shocked by the appearance of Vera, dressed in a moth-eaten fur coat, carrying an overnight case. She enters from the kitchen

Vera Hello. Who're you phoning? This time of night?

Isabel I was just—checking the time. It's late.

Vera Yes, I know. We sat up playing cards. And that sister-in-law of mine, she cheats. I could see it, and I told her. She didn't like it either. Accused me of being a bad loser. Right, I said. If that's how you feel. I'll never spend another night under this roof. Billy, I said, take me home. I know where my friends are. Is that chocolate there?

Isabel Yes, but it must be cold by now.

Vera That's all right. I'll soon heat it up. Won't take a jiff. You girls like some?

Aurelia Thank you, no.

Isabel No.

Vera Right.

Taking up the chocolate pot, Vera disappears into the kitchen

Aurelia looks with alarm at Isabel, who moves close to her and whispers

Isabel Don't panic. Listen. Those sleeping pills. I'll engage her attention. You make sure you put the pills in her chocolate. Then I'll pretend to go. If Mercer does come before she goes, I'll be able to cut him off. But when I go, you yawn and say you're tired, go upstairs. She won't stay here on her own. O.K.?

Aurelia Yes. O.K. (*She passes a hand over her eyes*) I don't know how you can think so quickly. My mind just blacks out...

Isabel (*quickly*) Shh...

Vera comes out of the kitchen into the room, with the chocolate pot

Vera There you are, what did I say, quick as jiff on the fast ring. (*She moves over to the table, pours herself a cup*) You girls sure you don't want any? (*Answering herself*) No, I see you didn't even finish the last lot.

Act 1, Scene 3

Isabel I tell you what I'd love. A nice biscuit. You haven't got one, have you, Vera?
Vera Oh, I think we might be able to oblige. (*To Aurelia*) What about you?
Aurelia No thanks.
Vera Back in a flash.

Vera goes into the kitchen

Isabel, keeping close to the kitchen door so as to block Vera's view if necessary, gestures hurriedly to Aurelia to put the pills in Vera's cup. Aurelia does so, just as Vera comes back

Vera enters with her usual charge from the kitchen, carrying a plate of biscuits

Isabel just times her move out of Vera's path to perfection

Vera There you are, love. Digestive. All right?
Isabel (*taking the biscuit*) Lovely. Then I must be going.

Isabel bites at the biscuit. Vera sits down and stirs her chocolate. Aurelia yawns

Aurelia I must go too. I feel exhausted. (*She yawns again*) Will you put the lights out, Vera?
Vera Don't worry about that. I'm going up myself right away. I've got a nice magazine, one of those new ones, you know, with all letters about sex problems. I like a read while I'm in bed, with a nice hot drink. I was only staying up with you to be sociable.
Isabel (*her mouth still full of biscuit*) Right—I'm off then. Good night, Vera. I'll see you tomorrow, Aurelia.
Aurelia Good night.
Isabel (*moving to the kitchen*) I'll go out the back way.

Isabel goes into the kitchen

Aurelia moves to the stairs, yawning. Vera rises.

Vera We might as well all go then. I'll take this up with me.
Aurelia All right, Vera. I'll see to the lights.
Vera (*moving to the stairs*) Will you, dear? And make sure the back door's double locked?
Aurelia (*moving back towards the kitchen*) Yes, I'll see to that now.
Vera (*yawning*) Oh, you've got me at it now. (*She starts to climb the stairs, halts*) Was that a car?
Aurelia What?
Vera I thought I heard a car stop outside.
Aurelia Who could it be, at this time of night?
Vera You never know, robbers.
Aurelia (*smiling*) If it is, I'll shoot them.

Vera (*smiling back*) Well do it quietly, love. We don't want to wake everyone up. Good night.
Aurelia Good night, Vera.

Vera continues up the stairs, out of sight, as Aurelia, pausing en route to turn off one of the standard lamps, moves into the kitchen. She returns after a moment's pause

Aurelia switches off the other lamps, leaving only the desk lamp. The rear porch light is still on, rendering the garden green, luminous, rather strange. Aurelia is lit by the remaining lamp. She stands there, downstage, motionless. Then she turns suddenly at a whisper. The rest of the stage is in darkness

Isabel enters from the kitchen, standing in the doorway. Mercer is behind her but we cannot see him in the darkness

Isabel (*from the kitchen door*) Has she gone?
Aurelia She's gone up. With her chocolate.
Isabel You'd better go up. Make sure she's gone to bed.
Aurelia Yes. Did he come?
Isabel He's here.
Mercer (*we cannot see him but hear his cheery whisper*) Evening.

Aurelia moves quickly to the stairs, goes up. We hear the creak of a floorboard upstairs

There is silence for a few moments, then, the sudden sound of a slap

Isabel (*in a fierce whisper*) You can cut that out.
Mercer (*cheerfully*) All right, darling. No offence.

A few moments' silence again, then the creak of the floorboard. Aurelia, a dim shadow, appears on the staircase. She hurries down, moves across to the kitchen, turning on a standard lamp en route

We see Isabel, with Mercer right behind her. Aurelia speaks to Isabel. Both converse in whispers

Aurelia Her door's shut, and she's snoring. I think she must have gone right off.
Isabel Did you look in on Lady Chalmont?
Aurelia Yes. She's fast asleep.

After their whispering, Mercer's voice is startling

Mercer Can we talk normally then?

Both women "shush" him

Isabel Yes, all right. But let's keep our voices down.
Mercer We can have one more light, can't we?

Aurelia looks at Isabel, who shrugs assent

Act I, Scene 3

I like to see who I'm doing business with.

Aurelia switches on the sofa table lamp

Especially when it's two beautiful ladies
Isabel All right, let's get down to business.
Mercer Oh come on—aren't you going to offer me a drink?
Isabel Do you want one?
Mercer (*hurt*) Not particularly. But I like to feel I'm being made welcome.
Isabel Well you're not. I'd give you a drink of arsenic if I had my way.
Mercer Well—you're this year's surprise result, aren't you—you looked as though butter wouldn't melt in your mouth—and now you're talking about murdering someone—just like her.
Aurelia The difference is with you it would be a pleasure.
Mercer (*sharply*) I'm sure. Indeed I'm quite aware of it. Which is why I've taken the necessary precautions. If anything happens to me, a certain sealed envelope will be winging its way immediately to the police—do you follow me?
Isabel I thought you'd think of something like that.
Mercer Got to think of everything in this business.
Aurelia That's all very well. But how do I know, if I pay you, that you'll keep quiet. As soon as you're short of money, you'll want paying again—and again—and again.
Mercer Ah, well now, that is the problem with blackmailers, as you might say. They are greedy and this does lead to all those Mr X cases you read about in the Sunday newspapers. I can only say that I'm not greedy and I am honest, in my own funny way.

Aurelia scoffs and turns away

Now come on, darling, fair's fair. I don't say I haven't had a few crooked dealings in my time, I have had, a fair few, and I'll go on having them because you've got to, all the people you deal with are crooks, like your late husband, to name but one. But tell me this, and tell the truth, you've known me a fair little time now, have you ever heard that I've cheated anybody, or not filled my part of a bargain? There's honour among thieves, you know, I sometimes think a lot more than there is among the so-called legitimate businessmen. You can believe it or not, and since you've got no choice, you might as well believe it—my word is my bond.
Aurelia (*with scorn*) Your word.
Isabel (*motioning her to be quiet*) All right. How much?
Mercer Well—I'll be reasonable—bearing in mind you're a widow and so on—and knowing that your husband didn't leave you all that well provided for. You've given me so far how much? In English money, about three thousand quid. I tell you what, no arguments, we'll say the balance up to twenty thousand. How's that?
Isabel (*with a gasp*) That's a fortune.
Mercer Oh come on. These days? It wouldn't buy a semi-detached in Surbiton.
Aurelia I told you. He'll bleed me for the rest of my life.

Mercer Turn it in. What is this, the local amateur dramatic society? I don't want to bleed you. It's no good, having money owed to you, if you've got to spend years collecting it. It's not worth my time. I'd rather take a small lump sum now, tax free, no problems, no pack drill. What d'you say?

Aurelia There's nothing I can say, but no. I just don't have that kind of money. It may be peanuts to you. But I would have to work a lifetime for it.

Mercer Depends on the kind of work. I mean, you're still a good looker, and a hostess in one of those West End clubs can pick up a nice bonus every now and then, you know, when a dolly sheikh comes in . . .

Aurelia (*fiercely*) I'm not whoring for you!

Isabel Be sensible, Mr Mercer. What you ask for is impossible. Let's talk in hundreds instead of thousands, and then we might come to a deal.

Mercer (*stung*) Hundreds? I can't even think in hundreds. This country's in the grip of raging inflation, didn't you know? I tell you, the working man in England is going to count his take-home pay in hundreds before long. And you're not going to equate me with a working man, I hope. I take a great pride in the fact that I have never done an honest day's work in all my life.

Isabel But look here . . .

Mercer (*angrily*) No, you look here. I mean, I may be a bit of a sucker for a beautiful bird, and you two are lovely ladies I must admit, but it doesn't soften my mind, I can still think straight. Just look around you, in this room where we're standing. Those pictures are early English impressionist, that china's old Spode, there's some good silver about and most of the furniture's genuine Victorian. I could get what I'm asking for the contents of this room alone and you accuse me of not being reasonable. I think that's a liberty, if you don't mind my saying so. And even if you do, I still think so.

Isabel But that's ridiculous. This house belongs to Lady Chalmont.

Mercer Her aunt.

Aurelia John's aunt.

Mercer John's dead. If anything happens to her, you inherit.

Aurelia John's not dead, not so far as the world knows.

Isabel And Lady Chalmont will probably live for years.

Mercer Not if she's helped on her way, she won't. Poor lady, she's already had one stroke. They told me, in the village.

Aurelia What are you trying to say, Mercer?

Mercer I wish you'd stop talking to me as if I were your butler. I'm not *trying* to say anything. I *am* saying. That your best bet is to knock off the old lady, whip the paintings and a few other valuables, make the whole job look like it was a gang of thieves. The time couldn't be better. They've had a few laggings round here recently.

Isabel (*aghast*) You mean *murder* her?

Mercer (*offended*) I like that! She *murders* her husband and you rally round to help. You talk about *murdering* me without a flutter of the eyebrows. But when I make a really constructive suggestion, to solve all our prob-

Act I, Scene 3

lems—and let's face it, she is an old lady who's past it, not someone in their prime like me—or John, come to that—when I propose a logical solution, we're all aghast at the awful morality of it all. I don't understand the middle classes, I really don't. I can make a living out of 'em but I'll never understand them, not really.

Aurelia (*wearily*) Let's stop this pantomime. I can't stand it any more. I'm so tired. All I want to do now is to sleep. And then tomorrow I'll give myself up, take my chances.

Isabel You can't.

Aurelia Well what do you propose? That I murder my aunt as he suggests?

Mercer Not you, dear. I never suggested you. Someone without a motive. Who's not going to benefit from the estate.

Aurelia (*clutching her head in bewilderment*) I don't know what you're saying —you've lost me. I just don't understand.

Isabel (*grimly*) Don't you? I do. He means me.

Mercer Clever girl. Listen, if you ever come to Africa, look me up. I'm sure we could do business together.

Aurelia He's mad.

Mercer I do resent that. I do, really.

Isabel Maybe, but there's an awful logic in his madness. Just one act— would solve everything.

Mercer You must be a Capricorn. Precise, logical, clear thinking. Just like me.

Isabel (*slowly*) It makes an incredible, terrifying—sense.

Aurelia (*with horror*) Isabel, what's happening to you? You're letting his madness affect you ...

Mercer I do wish people wouldn't make allusions like that. I don't like it.

Isabel (*as though in a dream*) No. I know what I'm doing.

Mercer (*to Isabel*) I'll tell you what I'll do, to show my good faith, I'll throw in the weapon as well. (*He puts a revolver on the table*) There you are, Colt thirty-eight, a child could use it, fully loaded, ready for action. Cost you a hundred quid or more in the East End, if you knew where to get one. I'll write it off, risk capital, what do you say?

Aurelia (*with sudden fury*) There's only one person I'd like to murder, and that's you ...

Aurelia rushes over to Mercer, attacks him. He falls back at first under the fury of her attack, then gets suddenly angry, hits her hard two or three times, beating her off. Isabel reaches for the gun, levels it at him

Isabel (*with authority*) Stop that!

Mercer (*straightening his rumpled clothing*) You want to tell her, not me. Marvellous, ain't it? You try to help people, and all they want to do is to attack you (*To Isabel*) When you're doing the job properly, make sure you release the safety catch. It's ever so embarrassing, pulling the trigger, when nothing happens. You feel a right fool, I can tell you.

Isabel looks down at the gun, then across to Aurelia, who has collapsed in a chair. Her body is shaking with her sobs

(*Backing towards the kitchen*) Yes, well—I'd better be going.

Isabel stares down at the gun again

That's right, the safety catch is that little thing just on the right there. Practise. But take the bullets out first. You might alarm someone.

Mercer reaches the kitchen door. Isabel is staring at him, the gun still in her hands, almost pointed at him

(*Nervously*) And do remember, never point the gun at anyone unless you intend to use it. That's what leads to accidents. It's quite straightforward, this job. All you have to remember is to smash a window and take a few paintings. Right—well—I'll leave you then . . . it's all coming and going this evening, isn't it? Good night, then. (*He glances at Aurelia who is still sobbing*) Say good night to your friend . . .

And Mercer vanishes, into the kitchen

Isabel turns back slowly, to look at Aurelia. Her movements are dreamlike. Aurelia, sobbing, raises her face to Isabel. She seems horrified by what she sees

Aurelia Isabel—what are you doing with that gun? What's happened to you?

The lights start to dim rapidly to a single spot on Isabel

Isabel I don't know. But something. (*Staring down at the gun, whispering to herself*) Something!

The spot fades to a Black-out

Scene 4

The same. Several days later

The scene opens in darkness. After a pause, three shots are heard, followed by the sound of breaking glass. After another pause, the Lights come up. It is a sunny morning, but there is an atmosphere of sadness about the house. The room looks bare, denuded of its pictures and some of its bric-a-brac

There is the sound of a car drawing up and stopping, then the front door opens and closes. A woman is heard sobbing, off. Vera enters, sobbing, comforted by Aurelia. Both are dressed in black

Aurelia There now—there—look, you sit down. I'll make you a cup of tea or something . . .

Vera Yes—all right—(*sitting*)—I'd better have something—a little brandy perhaps . . . ?

Aurelia All right.

Aurelia moves to pour Vera a brandy. Vera continues to sniffle

Vera Not too much. Doctor says I shouldn't drink at all. But it's not every

Act I, Scene 4

day you attend the funeral of your dearest friend. (*As Aurelia brings her drink across to her*) I wasn't just an employee here, you know.

Aurelia I know. Lady Chalmont told me many times how fond she was of you.

Aurelia's words kick off renewed tears

Vera I reproach myself. I do. If I hadn't forgiven that awful sister-in-law of mine, and gone back to my brother's place that night, it might never have happened.

Aurelia The gang—or whoever it was—might have shot you as well, Vera. We could all think, as you do, if only we had been here. But we weren't. I was in Oxford, at a concert. I reproach myself too. It's natural. But not logical. Now come on, sip your brandy...

Vera I shouldn't. I really shouldn't. (*She downs the brandy in the glass with one practised gulp*)

Aurelia (*drily*) Have another. (*She takes Vera's glass*)

Vera Well perhaps just one more sip. I've been under the doctor, you know, ever since this happened. It brought on palpitations. Terrible. He says I've got to take life very easily.

Aurelia (*coming back with another drink*) Then that's what you'll have to do. I can manage around the house until—well it'll be sold soon, I imagine. So why don't you stay on at your brother's place, take it easy?

Vera I will. I must. This has all been such a shock to me.

Aurelia It's been a shock to us all.

Vera I thought I was getting over it, until the funeral today. Then it all started up again, my palpitations and all. When I saw the coffin—(*sniffing*) and I knew she was in there—(*sniffing*) I thought I'd faint.

Aurelia Well you were very brave. And it all went off well, didn't it?

Vera Oh yes. It was a lovely funeral. And so many people there. It makes you think, doesn't it? I bet there wouldn't have been a quarter of them if the poor dear had passed away natural. People are morbid. D'you know that? Morbid.

Aurelia Yes. They love tragedy, don't they? I've never seen so many people at a funeral. And I hardly knew one of them.

Vera I knew most. By sight, anyway. Not that they had any rights to be there. Just being morbid and nosey, they were. And there were quite a few police...

Aurelia (*surprised*) Police?

Vera Oh yes—they were looking everyone over—looking for the murderer, I suppose...

Aurelia But I thought—(*with forced casualness*)—I thought they suspected the Hell's Angels, or whatever you call them.

Vera I don't know. They didn't confide in me. Questioned me, though. Gave me quite a grilling. Didn't they you?

Aurelia Well, yes. But it was just routine. It never crossed my mind that— you know...

Vera Oh yes. They suspect everyone, the C.I.D. do. You can't blame 'em, can you? I mean, that's their job.

Aurelia (*forcing a smile*) It's a good thing we both have good alibis, isn't it? Do you know, that really shocks me, the thought of police at the funeral. I don't know why.

Vera It's not so much those who were there, as those who weren't, that shocks me, if you know what I mean.

Aurelia Isabel?

Vera After everything my lovely lady did for her. Treated her like a daughter. And then not to show respect.

Aurelia You mustn't think that. Isabel's been dreadfully ill since it happened. She's had a real nervous breakdown. So you can hardly say she didn't care for Lady Chalmont.

Vera She couldn't have cared more that I did. But I kept going. And I've got palpitations.

Aurelia Yes, but Isabel is such a nervous, imaginative child. The sudden death of someone close can—unhinge—someone like that.

Vera (*unconvinced*) Yes, well—I expect you're right. But I know what they'll be saying in the village—that she kept away from the funeral because she wasn't left anything in the will.

Aurelia (*in a shocked tone*) But that's an awful thing to say.

Vera You know what people are like. It's the only topic of conversation at the moment. I mean they all knew that John was sort of kicked out of the house. And now he inherits the lot—(*she shrugs*)—they think it's a bit funny.

Aurelia Well I wish they'd mind their own business. John was Lady Chalmont's only living relative. That's why he inherits. Why should Isabel? She wasn't related.

Vera No. Quite. I'm just telling you what people say. I mean, I gave my lady twenty years of devoted service. Some of the best years of my life. I could have got married again. But I stayed loyal. Because that's my character. Not for any expectations. But I wouldn't have missed going to that funeral today. I know what people would have said.

Aurelia I know how devoted you were to Lady Chalmont and, I promise you, when the estate is cleared up, I shan't forget you.

Vera Oh thank you. I knew I could rely on you. (*She gets up*) I feel much better now. Would you like me to make you a cup of coffee before I go off?

Aurelia Er—yes. That might be nice.

The telephone rings and Vera turns from her passage to the kitchen to answer it

Vera Hello? Yes. Yes, who's calling? Just a minute. (*She puts down the phone*) Mr Mercer.

Vera exits to the kitchen

Aurelia Thank you. (*She waits until Vera has gone, then picks up the phone*) Hello? Yes . . . You were in Paris? . . . Yes, it was a great shock to all of us . . . I, er, haven't seen her . . . Police believe it was a gang. (*She listens a moment, keeping her eye on the kitchen*) The account? Oh yes, I'll settle

Act I, Scene 4

that as soon as I clear things up . . . (*Nodding*) Not at all. Thank you for calling. Good-bye. (*She puts the phone down, smiling slightly, then is suddenly startled as she notices Isabel*)

Isabel appears at the open garden door. She is dressed all in black, but not in any formal sense. Her clothes have just been thrown on. She wears no make-up and her hair is untidy. She has dark circles under her eyes and looks deathly pale

Before either of them can say anything, and as Isabel steps into the room, Vera comes bustling out from the kitchen

Vera I thought I saw someone in the gar . . . (*She breaks off as she sees Isabel and immediately goes to her*) Oh, you poor love—here, come and sit down —I'll fetch you a nice cup of coffee. (*As she seats Isabel*) Look at her, poor darling, she's trembling . . .
Isabel (*haltingly*) I'm all right. But I have been ill. (*To Vera*) Thank you . . . I'd love some coffee.
Vera Right . . .

Vera exits to the kitchen

Isabel waits for Vera to go

Isabel You didn't come to see me.
Aurelia (*calmly*) I enquired. They said it was better for you not to see anyone.
Isabel It's been like a nightmare. I don't know how I've lived these last few days. I've got to tell someone about it, or I'll go mad. And there's no-one to talk to, Aurelia, except you.
Aurelia You'll be all right. Why don't you take a little holiday? Don't worry about how much it costs.
Isabel (*keeping her voice down, glancing towards the kitchen*) What happened? Did you see Mercer again?
Aurelia Mercer? Who's Mercer?
Isabel (*in a fierce whisper*) The blackmailer!
Aurelia Darling, what are you talking about? You're still delirious.
Isabel (*holding back her tears*) Please—Aurelia—what are you trying to do to me? Don't make it any worse or I'll go mad, completely . . . (*She breaks off, sobbing*)

Vera enters with the coffee tray.

Aurelia Isabel, I really think you should get home as soon as you've had your drink, and call the doctor. You're not well yet. You're still imagining things. I'm sorry if I seem unsympathetic, but it's been very bad for us too, and we've had to carry on. John and I have a tremendous number of problems in clearing up the estate and . . .
Isabel Who? Who did you say?

Aurelia looks up as the visitor, a handsome young man dressed in black, enters the room, behind Isabel

Aurelia (*calmly*) Oh darling, there you are—look who's come to see us.
John (*easily*) Hello, Isabel. (*He smiles at Vera*) Hello, Vera.

Isabel rises and stands staring at John, in a state of complete shock. John takes off the black topcoat which he wears. As he does so, he talks to Isabel quite normally

It's lovely to see you again—but what an awful occasion. God, I hate funerals. And this morning—shaking hands with all those people—saying the same stupidly polite things over and over again—it's so tiring. (*Divested of his coat, he moves towards Isabel, opening his arms to greet her*) I feel dead.

Isabel falls in a faint on the floor, as—

the CURTAIN *falls*

ACT II

Scene 1

The same. Immediately following

John picks up Isabel and, aided by Vera, puts her on to a nearby couch. Aurelia watches them, a slight smile on her face

Vera I think there's some smelling salts upstairs in the bathroom. I'll go and have a look.

Vera exits upstairs

Aurelia moves to look down on Isabel, the same cynical smile on her face. John, who looks genuinely concerned, loosens the neck of Isabel's dress

John She's fainted.
Aurelia I didn't think she'd had a heart attack. Worse luck. (*Gesturing to him*) Mind where your hands go.
John Don't be ridiculous. I've never ever seen anyone go out cold like that. It must have been one hell of a shock for her.
Aurelia You returning from the dead? I'm sure. I mean who next? Maybe her victim.
John (*shaking his head*) I just can't believe that of Isabel. I really can't.
Aurelia Well it's true and the proof will soon be lining our pockets. Your sweet and innocent little Isabel did everything I told her—in fact, more.
John What is it about you? Are you some kind of witch?
Aurelia Well that's one of the nicer names I've been called. It wasn't so difficult. It's just a matter of playing on people's weak spots. And you know Isabel's great weakness?
John No.
Aurelia You. She had this memory of you locked away in her heart like a pressed flower—this sweet and innocent love for you. When your wicked auntie sent you away—which you well deserved, my pet, as you know—it was like a child having her favourite toy ripped away from her. I sensed that immediately with your darling Isabel.
John She was so young—still in her teens . . .
Aurelia I know. I said so. A child. Emotionally, anyway. Even if she was developed in other directions—I knew inside little Miss Goody-two-shoes there was a burning cauldron of hate. All I had to do was to find it and stir it.
John You missed your vocation.
Aurelia You mean I should have been a psychiatrist? I think you're right. I seem to know instinctively what makes people tick. I find, whenever I

read articles on psychology, that I understand them immediately, even long words I've never heard before. I just seem to understand the logic of it.

John rises from his kneeling position, looks down at Isabel

John Poor kid.

Aurelia Like with Isabel. Deep down, there was a simmering hate of the old lady, despite the weekly calls, the tea and cucumber sandwiches. I brought it out. And deep down, there was the love for you. And that I killed.

John Did you?

Aurelia Yes. By killing you. I made myself your *alter ego* first, so that she would love me. And then I took the image of you, the one she was so scared of, the bad boy image with all the threats that it carried, and I killed it for her. By that time, she wanted me to kill it. She even wanted to help me.

John You've lost me.

Aurelia It was all beautifully symbolic. We had to bury your body. So I did in the quicksands at the back of the plantation.

John (*angrily*) I don't know what the hell you're talking about.

Aurelia (*calmly*) Listen, and you'll find out. By now, I had killed the bad boy, and I was substitute for the good one. And so she loved me. And to love someone is to be in their power.

John (*pacing the room*) I wish to hell you'd never done it. (*He stops, faces her angrily*) Why? We never discussed anything like this.

Aurelia (*coldly*) We discussed our monetary problems and we knew there was only one way out, for your aunt to die. You were too much of a coward to kill her yourself, but you didn't care how I arranged it. So I did.

John I didn't mean——

Aurelia —me to use Isabel? I know. But you don't tell your doctor how to prescribe or your mechanic how to fix your car. I did the job my way, and cleverly, if I say so myself.

John (*bitterly*) Oh yes . . .

Aurelia Yes. Murder by proxy. When I'd sprung the trap, I set the bait. My life, my freedom, was suddenly in danger when a mysterious blackmailer appeared . . .

John Who the hell was that?

Aurelia Our friend Freddy. The one they call the actor. (*As he frowns*) Don't worry, he's got a reputation. He's been mixed up in murder before this.

John Do you have to keep saying that word?

Aurelia Well, what else? Why not call a spade a spade?

John shrugs and turns away

You might as well listen, because you're an accomplice. You're just as guilty as I am. (*In a hard tone*) I was the bait. My love for her. Her love for me. That was what was at risk. And the only way out was to kill your dear aunt.

John *(turning)* I don't want to hear all this.
Aurelia You'll hear it and like it. That night, I put the gun in her hand. I told her exactly what she had to do. She was in a trance, almost as though I had hypnotized her. *(Cynically)* And then I drove like hell away from here, to establish an alibi. Even the police co-operated with me. I got a ticket for speeding.
John *(looking down at Isabel)* But what now? Now she knows she's been tricked?
Aurelia The poor little cow will have to live with her own conscience. Or blab it all out and be locked away in a lunatic asylum.
John God, you're a hard bitch.
Aurelia *(sweetly)* Only when my territory is threatened. I know how much she cared for you and, now I've seen you look at her, I know it wasn't all one-sided.

John passes a hand over his eyes

What's the matter?
John I don't know. I feel dizzy.
Aurelia Christ, don't you start fainting.
John I mean sick. Sick to my stomach. For Christ's sake, Aurelia, what the hell's happened to us? What have we become?
Aurelia *(in a hard voice)* Rich, baby. That's what we've become. And that's how we're going to stay. Together. Because we've got a bond now. Of sentiment. The memory of your dear aunt.
John You're a—monster!
Aurelia That's right. A monster. With intelligence and cunning. And you're a monster, too. But lazy and gutless.
John *(bitterly)* What are you trying to say? That we were made for each other?
Aurelia Something like that. That you were made for me, anyway. And while we're here, you just remember that. You're mine. *(Her tone changes abruptly, becomes all sweet)* Why Vera, we were just going to send out a search party.

Vera appears on the stairs, grumbling and carrying a bottle of smelling salts

Vera That's what you need, in that bathroom. The number of boxes and bottles we've stored up over the years is unbelievable. You could start a shop with them. I began to think my memory was playing me tricks, that we had everything you could think of except smelling salts. And then I found them. *(She reaches the foot of the stairs and heads straight for the couch, unscrewing the top of the smelling salts bottle)* My goodness, she still hasn't come round. You were quite right. We really will have to send her home and call a doctor. *(She passes the salts under Isabel's nose)*
Aurelia You know, it's just occurred to me—I bet she came here without telling anyone—if they've found she's missing, they'll be worried as hell—why don't you just pop across and tell them? *(She takes the smelling salts from Vera)* I'll do that.

Vera (*rising, perturbed*) Oh—poor dear . . . (*To John*) She is going to be all right, isn't she?
John (*soothingly*) Yes—she'll be fine.

Vera moves to the kitchen, but slowly. She seems reluctant to leave

Vera Only—I'd be very—upset—if anything happened to Isabel.
John (*quietly*) We all would, Vera.
Aurelia But if you meet anyone from the village, don't say anything. We don't want Isabel to be the next subject of gossip, just because the poor darling's had a breakdown.
Vera (*at the door*) Course not. (*She sobs*) I'll be as silent as the grave. (*She sobs*) Oh, what have I said?

Vera rushes through into the kitchen

A pause, then we hear the back door slam. John frowns after Vera, then turns to Aurelia

John What was that about? She doesn't suspect anything, does she?
Aurelia No. Why should she? Don't worry about her. I've promised her a little legacy.

During this last exchange, Isabel, on the couch, opens her eyes. She raises herself on her elbow and both of them turn towards her as they hear her stir

Isabel (*her voice hoarse*) You've been clever, haven't you? Really clever? You've got everyone squared.
Aurelia Don't worry, dear. We won't leave you out.
Isabel You bitch!
Aurelia (*mockingly*) And not a week ago, she loved me.
Isabel I loved John, not you.
John Isabel—please—I want you to know . . .
Isabel (*turning on him, with loathing*) I don't want to know anything from you. You're as bad as she is.
Aurelia (*amused*) That's what I keep telling him. We were made for each other.
John Look, there's no point in my trying to hide anything. I'm in this as deep as she is, and as deep as she says you are. But I want you to know—if it's only for old times' sake—that I never knew you'd be involved. It was all Aurelia's idea, one hundred per cent.
Aurelia You can play down your role as much as you like. The fact is, when it comes to the final scene, you're right up there alongside me, sharing the benefits from what we've done. You don't mind the glory of the curtain-call, do you, darling? It's all the hard graft that goes before, that puts you off.
John (*turning away*) I don't want a penny from this—mess!
Aurelia (*cynically*) Would you like to put that in writing?
Isabel (*to Aurelia*) You think you can manipulate everyone, don't you?
Aurelia I know who I can, and who I can't.
Isabel You mean people like us.

Act II, Scene 1

Aurelia You can cut out that bracketing yourself with John. He's mine now. We have only one link, the three of us, that we're all accomplices. It doesn't matter how, or why: whether it was—*(to John, who flinches)*—cowardice, or—*(to Isabel)*—naïveté. But that's what we are. And only we know it. If this ever got to court, it was Isabel's finger on the trigger, and no-one else's.

John turns slowly, miserably, to face Aurelia

John Why? Why did you have to pick on her?
Aurelia *(ignoring him, questioning Isabel)* Did you get rid of the gun?
Isabel *(after a pause)* Yes. In the river.
Aurelia No-one saw you?
Isabel No-one.
Aurelia The paintings?
Isabel *(after a pause)* I destroyed them.
Aurelia Good. Then we'll have no problems with the insurance. *(To John)* See? Your sweet little Isabel did the job more efficiently than I would have done.

Isabel sits up

Congratulations, dear.
Isabel That's all right. *(She stares at Aurelia)* Just pay me.
Aurelia *(stunned)* What?
Isabel *(in a hard voice)* I did what you asked. You've reaped the reward. Now share it.
John Isabel!
Isabel What are you sounding so shocked about?
Aurelia *(enjoying this)* Right. What did I tell you, John? I ought to get an honorary degree or something. A complete personality change.
Isabel Never mind about that. How much?
Aurelia I think we might scrape together a thousand.
Isabel Who do you think you are kidding? Those paintings alone are insured for thirty-five thousand. And don't tell me they're not, because I arranged it.
Aurelia All right. Five thousand. But that's it.
Isabel I want twenty-five. And I won't settle for a penny less.
Aurelia Oh? What are you going to do? Go to the police?
Isabel I might. Or to the Sunday papers. They like a good scandal.
Aurelia There is a law of libel, you know. What are you going to tell them? About my dead husband? Who's walking around? Or the blackmailer Mercer? Who doesn't exist? Newspapers—and the police for that matter—want facts. All you've got is a very tall story.
Isabel You please yourself. But I'm not bluffing. I don't know exactly how I'll break it, and when I do work it out, I'm not going to tell you. But so far as I'm concerned, there's nothing to lose and, for all your alibis, I swear if I go to prison, I'll take you with me. Both!

There is a long pause. It is a true moment of bluff, and of decision. It is John who breaks first

John Aurelia, we've got enough. Pay Isabel what she wants.
Aurelia Shut up.

John shuts up. The two women continue to stare at each other

Isabel I'm not bluffing.
Aurelia There's only one way to test that, isn't there? And that's to call your hand.
Isabel Call it.
Aurelia (*after a pause*) All right. Twenty-five thousand. But only when the insurance company pays up.
Isabel That will do.
Aurelia All right. That's settled. Now you can get the hell out of here.
Isabel No.
Aurelia (*astonished*) What?
Isabel I think we should keep up pretences, don't you? I mean, people in the village would expect me to rally round, to stay here and look after my dear friends in their awful tragedy.
Aurelia (*with her eyes narrowed*) Why, really, do you want to stay here?
Isabel To keep an eye on my inheritance.
Aurelia Is that all?
Isabel (*sweetly*) Don't you trust me? I'm surprised at you, Aurelia, being so uncertain of yourself.
Aurelia (*curtly*) I'm certain, of everything I do.
Isabel That's all right then. You don't mind, do you, John?
John (*startled at suddenly being included*) Me? No.
Aurelia (*grimly*) No.

Isabel smiles sweetly at her. Aurelia is about to make some biting reply

Vera comes huffing and puffing in

Vera Oh—I haven't done so much running about in years. I'll be the next one to go down if I'm not careful. (*To Isabel*) Thank heavens you're back on your feet...
Isabel Yes, I feel fine now, Vera. I'm sorry if I've been a trouble to you...
Vera No trouble to me, love...
Isabel I know I have been to dear Aurelia...
Aurelia (*forcing a smile*) Of course not.
Isabel (*in a breathless little girl voice*) But now I'm going to try hard to make it up to everyone. I'm going to stay here and help you with the housework, Vera, and do everything I can to help John and Aurelia in this trying time.
Vera (*genuinely admiring*) Isn't that nice? (*Her face changing*) But I've just been telling your parents how ill you are, and how you should come straight home and go to bed.
Isabel That's all right, Vera. I'll go across now and explain to them how much better I feel. (*To John*) Perhaps you would be kind enough to come with me, John, and bring my case back here. I still feel a little weak.

Act II, Scene 1   45

Aurelia makes a face, turns away. John looks at her appealingly but she has her back to him

John Er—yes—of course . . .
Isabel (*in her little girl voice*) We'll go out through the garden, shall we? It's so lovely there, and peaceful. It makes one forget all the awful things that have happened.

Isabel goes to the garden door. John, with a last glance at Aurelia, which is unacknowledged, follows

(*As she goes*) And Mummy and Daddy will be so pleased to see you. We can talk about old times . . .

Isabel and John exit, their voices fade away

Vera beams with a kind of proprietorial pride after them

Vera They make a lovely couple, don't they. (*With a chuckle*) I meant no offence, miss . . .
Aurelia He's nearer her age than I am to his, if that's what you meant to point out.
Vera There, I have offended you. And I didn't intend that at all. You must remember that I've known them since they were both children.
Aurelia Yes, I'm well aware of it. In fact, the cloying sentimentality of this place is driving me mad.
Vera Well—you'll be leaving it soon. I have to stay here—which reminds me—do you think we could have our little chat now?
Aurelia Our little chat? What about?
Vera (*delicately*) Well, the, er, provision.
Aurelia What?
Vera What we were talking about. From the estate.
Aurelia Oh—that—well I really can't say at the moment . . .
Vera Only I'm getting on now, you know . . .
Aurelia (*impatiently*) Yes.
Vera And being under the doctor and everything, you understand, I don't really want to go round searching for another job, not at my time of life.
Aurelia Yes, well, perhaps we could talk about it later.
Vera I hope you don't mind my raising the matter but I wasn't sure what you had in mind . . .
Aurelia (*trying to close the conversation*) I'm really not sure myself, Vera. I'll have to think about it.
Vera Well yes, of course, and I have to think about it too. I was talking it over with my brother a few days ago and of course his children are growing up now, they want rooms of their own. And he mentioned that little cottage just along the road from him. It's up for sale, going quite cheap they say.
Aurelia (*frowning*) A cottage? Well, I wasn't really thinking of anything like that—how much is it?
Vera (*promptly*) Fifteen thousand.

Aurelia A cottage!

Vera I know, it's awful, isn't it, the way everything's gone up? Who'd have believed they'd ever have the cheek to ask fifteen thousand pounds for a cottage? Mind you, it's very nice, I believe. Got central heating and double glazing, and all that.

Aurelia And fitted carpets and gold plated taps, I should think, for that price. I'm sorry, Vera, but that's out of the question . . .

Vera (*unperturbed*) Well I leave it to you, you have a think about it. It's very difficult to make decisions, unless you think about them carefully, isn't it? I worried myself silly, for days you know, wondering if I ought to say anything about that Mr Mercer . . .

Aurelia (*sharply*) Mercer?

Vera Yes, you know, the gentleman who telephoned here today, and who came to visit you that night, when I came back from my brother's place. (*Chuckling*) You thought I was asleep, didn't you, when you came up? But that chocolate was too bitter tasting for me, and I was just putting on that snoring when you listened at my door. You can hear anyone come up the stairs here, you know, it's that creaking board.

Aurelia (*staring at her as though she were a ghost*) My god . . .

Vera (*without any change of amicable tone*) Anyway, like I was saying, prices are sky high. But as my brother says, it's all relative. If that cottage is worth fifteen thousand, he says, think how much Lady Chalmont's house would fetch. I've no idea, I said, it's none of my business, but it must be worth that little cottage a few times over. (*She sighs*) Oh dear, I do go on, don't I, I'm always being told about it, and yet the funny thing is, people don't know how silent I can be. Like I said before, silent as the grave, only this time it's not a slip of the tongue, if you know what I mean. (*She picks up the coffee cups, puts them on the tray*) What a shame, no-one drank their coffee. Never mind, I'll make some more—it's all been a bit dramatic, hasn't it? Perhaps it'll soothe our nerves a bit . . .

And Vera goes off into the kitchen with the tray, leaving Aurelia open-mouthed

Aurelia transfers her stare downstage. She looks shattered

Aurelia (*ticking them off on her fingers*) Isabel—Mercer—Vera . . . (*Her gesture plainly questions: what is going to be left for her?*)

The lights fade to a Black-out

SCENE 2

The same. Several nights later

The curtains are open. John and Isabel are sitting on the sofa, slightly apart, watching television. They are holding coffee cups, and the debris of a fork supper lies on the coffee table. Vera comes in from the kitchen and moves to collect the plates

Act II, Scene 2   47

Vera How was the chocolate cake, all right?
Isabel Lovely, thanks.
John (*agreeing*) Mmm.
Vera Good. I made that myself. From a recipe in the paper. I'm glad you liked it. I've left some in the fridge, by the way, for Aurelia.
John Right.
Vera Although I expect she's had supper out.
John (*with a glance at his watch*) I don't know. It's early yet.
Vera It might be for you. It's not for me. I've been at it all day. And so has poor Aurelia. Today and every day. You've got to hand it to her. She gets things done.
John Yes. She certainly does.
Vera I know what it's like, having to deal with solicitors. We had it when my Uncle Alf died. The way they hang on to the money, you'd think it was theirs. And the bank is just as bad. No wonder they've got all those assets you read about. I reckon it's all dead people's money they're holding on to, without paying any interest.
John You may be right.
Vera Anyway, I'd rather her than me. Right, that's it then. I'll just wash this little lot up and then I'll be getting off, if that's all right by you.
Isabel That's fine Vera. Thank you.

Vera exits

Isabel and John are still sitting slightly apart, hardly ever taking their glance from the screen, as though they were enrapt at whatever programme is (softly) playing. But as soon as Vera goes through the kitchen door, with perfect timing, they close in on each other for a deep kiss. It is John who breaks away

John Be careful. She might come in.
Isabel I'm tired of being careful.
John You're right. What does it matter if she does see us, and goes nattering to Aurelia? The sooner we fetch this business to a head, the better.

John kisses Isabel but now it is her turn to pull away

Isabel No, I'm being silly, emotional. It's better that she doesn't know—not yet.
John Why? What difference does it make, when she knows?
Isabel I don't know. But Aurelia's not somebody you want to upset unnecessarily. We can wait. So long as I know you love me. And you know I love you.
John That's the only thing that makes this nightmare bearable. I think for the first time in my life, in spite of all the terrible circumstances, I've found true happiness. I loved you before but—well I was always kind of sidetracked by other things, my so-called friends, drinking, gambling, all that. I never wanted to burden you with my weaknesses. But now it's happened and I didn't make it happen. Strangely enough, Aurelia did.

But she put you to the test for me, without knowing it. And what you did, you did for me. Aurelia always used my weakness, encouraged it in a way so that she could always control me. But you understand me, you have a compassion for me that she never had. When I'm with you, I feel whole. With Aurelia, I'm just a fragment of her personality.

Isabel But you fell in love with her. You married her.

John Yes. But remember what it was like for me when I first went out there. I'd left here in disgrace, lucky not to be sent to prison. My father's plantation was a wreck and I knew I'd be lucky to earn a living from it. And then I met Aurelia. When I was in pieces. She put me back together again. I must give her credit for that. But she put me back the way she wanted so that I was her puppet. Always she pulled the strings, and I danced. I worked damned hard on the plantation to try to make a go of it, but it wasn't enough for her. She wanted money and the bright lights and so she went off to be a hostess in a club, and I was supposed to stomach that. She would probably have left me if we hadn't had a stroke of luck, if world trade hadn't suddenly turned our way. We started to make a bit of money at last, and I wanted to plough it back into the business. But not Aurelia. Oh no, it was good times, visits to the city, parties, champagne suppers, days at the races. And when trade turned against us again, instead of being cushioned for it, we were almost broke. That was when she came up with her plan for coming to England. I swear I didn't know what she had in mind. You must know Aurelia by now, you can imagine how she put it to me. I've got a plan, she said. All you have to do is to go along with it, with every detail.

John turns his head away in shame. Isabel caresses him sympathetically

If you're weak, like me, you're done for. When she told me, I could do no more about it than a fly on that ceiling. She knew that. All I could do was go along with her. Along whatever road she chose.

Isabel You'll find strength.

John (*turning back to her*) I already have. In you. You only have to say the word and I will tell Aurelia tonight, that we love each other. I'm not afraid of her any more.

Isabel It's not a matter of being afraid. But of being careful. She's dangerous. And she'll fight against this tooth and claw. I mean it, John. We must take her seriously. That's why I don't want to rush into this. She'll do everything in her power to destroy us.

John Let her.

Isabel You're courageous now.

John Because of you.

It is a close intimate moment which, with perfect timing, they both break away from on cue, a split second before Vera makes her entrance

Vera comes in from the kitchen, pulling on her topcoat

Vera There we are. All done. I'll just see if there's anything Aurelia wants, and then I'll go.

Act II, Scene 2

Isabel (*surprised*) Is she here?
Vera Yes. She came in the back way. (*She chuckles*) Perhaps she was trying to surprise us?

John and Isabel glance quickly at each other. They edge apart, on the couch.

Aurelia enters from the kitchen

Aurelia (*to Vera*) Hello? Still here?
Vera Yes. I hung on to see if there was anything you wanted?
Aurelia (*removing her coat*) No, thank you. I had a snack while I was out.
Vera There's some chocolate cake in the fridge. And hot coffee in the pot.
Aurelia Something a bit stronger, I think. I've had a hard day.
John (*half rising*) Can I . . .
Aurelia (*moving to the drinks tray*) No, it's all right. I'll get it myself. (*She pours a drink*) What have you two been doing?
Isabel Not much. Just watching T.V.
Aurelia Well I've been slogging my guts out, if you'll pardon the inelegant phrase.
Vera How'd you get on, miss? All right?
Aurelia Eventually. I managed to pin them down in the end, for a substantial advance, at least.
John When?
Aurelia Two weeks.
Vera Oh, well that's nice. I mean, anyone who's going to benefit can make plans, can't they?
Aurelia Yes, they can. And, Vera, that reminds me. We'd better have a little chat this evening. About your notice, and severance pay, and so on.
Vera All right, miss. I'll hang on then, shall I?
Aurelia If you don't mind.
Vera Sure you wouldn't like a snack?
Aurelia I haven't eaten since lunch, I must admit.
Vera I'll get you something.

Vera goes off into the kitchen

Aurelia sips her drink, turns her attention to John and Isabel. John gets up to switch off the television, and moves the set back

Aurelia Don't turn it off for me.
Isabel It was boring, anyway.
Aurelia No more than me, I'm sure. Why don't you go out? It's quite mild.
John Out? Where?
Aurelia Don't ask me. It's your home town. Why not go to the pictures. There's a good murder on. With a sex film as second feature. I can't think of anything more appropriate.
John (*angrily*) Now look . . .
Isabel (*silencing him with a gesture*) That's right. I saw the poster. It's a Hitchcock picture. All about an evil woman who gets her comeuppance.

And the film with it is—a romance. Not even an X certificate, sorry to disappoint you. It sounds quite a good programme. Shall we go?
John (*glancing at Aurelia*) Er—well . . .
Isabel (*sweetly*) It was Aurelia's suggestion.
Aurelia That's right.
John All right. Why not?
Aurelia Why not indeed?
Isabel (*rising*) I'll just get my coat.

Isabel exits upstairs

John watches Isabel run up the stairs, then turns to Aurelia

John You're throwing me at her. Why? What's the game?
Aurelia (*wearily*) The same game it's always been. I know that this way, you get over it quickly. Remember? The waitress at that restaurant? The air hostess? The little blonde at the bank? None of them lasted a fortnight. So far as I'm concerned, the sooner you bed your childhood sweetheart the better, the quicker you'll be disillusioned and we'll have done with it. None of them come up to scratch in bed, do they, Johnny? Remember? How you used to tell me all about it?
John That's all over. It's different now.
Aurelia (*mockingly*) Is it?
John Yes, it is. And if you don't believe me, let me tell you something . . .
Aurelia Yes?

John starts to speak, but stops when he hears Isabel coming

Isabel comes down the stairs with her coat on

Isabel I'm ready. Won't you take a coat?
John (*after a pause*) Yes. It's in the hall.
Aurelia Good night then. I'll probably be in bed by the time you come back.
Isabel Good night.

John and Isabel start to leave

Vera enters with a plate of food

Vera Oh? Going out?
John Yes. Good night.
Aurelia (*as they leave*) Have fun.

John and Isabel exit through the dining-room

Vera (*serving Aurelia*) Here.
Aurelia Vera—I know you'll hate me—but suddenly I can't stand the sight of food.
Vera (*taking the plate away*) That's all right. I understand.

Act II, Scene 2

Aurelia God, I must have lost half a stone this last couple of weeks.
Vera Well it's the strain. Are you sure I can't get you anything?
Aurelia Quite sure. Just come and talk to me. Have a drink.
Vera (*pleased*) Oh—that'd be nice. Doctor says I shouldn't, mind.
Aurelia What do doctors know about it?
Vera That's true. I've never known anyone sink more than my doctor. (*As she exits*) I think he advises people not to drink so as to make sure there are always adequate supplies for him.

Vera goes into the kitchen

Aurelia smiles wryly as Vera goes. She consults her wristwatch, seems satisfied by what she sees

Vera returns

Vera Right then. Just a social one while we have our chat, and then I really must be going.
Aurelia What can I get you?
Vera That's all right. I'll help myself. (*She moves to the drinks tray and pours*) It looks as though I might be all right for that cottage then?
Aurelia Yes, Vera, I think you're in luck.
Vera Oh, I am pleased. I've got a feeling that I shall be very happy there. And you must come and visit me whenever you want.
Aurelia (*ironically*) That's what they call a paying guest, is it?
Vera Eh? (*She sees the joke, chuckles*) Oh, you are a card, you really are...

Both women gasp as, quite suddenly, the Lights go out. We can just see the silhouette of their figures against the picture window. The garden beyond is lit by a watery moon

It must be a fuse. The box is on the landing. I'll see if I...
Aurelia (*as Vera moves towards her*) Sh! Listen!

The sound of dragging footsteps is heard, the tap of a cane

Vera (*clutching her throat*) Oh, my god, what is it?
Aurelia There's someone on the stairs. I can hear them.
Vera It's her. (*Her voice rising*) It's her!
Aurelia Look!

Aurelia screams and points up the stairs. Vera screams and throws her arms round Aurelia

On the staircase we see a shimmering object, like the ghost of Lady Chalmont, tapping its way down the stairs.

Aurelia (*panicking*) You're right. It's her. Oh, God!
Vera (*her voice a painful croak*) My heart. It won't stand it. Help me—help me...

Vera falls to her knees, still holding on to Aurelia, weeping. Aurelia tries to free herself

Aurelia (*to the ghost*) No—please—it wasn't me...

The ghost of Lady Chalmont is at the foot of the stairs. It raises a revolver and points it at Aurelia. Vera is choking with fear. Aurelia's voice rises to a scream

It wasn't me!

Aurelia moves as though to attack the ghost. The ghost fires. Aurelia falls to the floor. The ghost turns and points the revolver at the whimpering Vera

Vera (*painfully forcing out each word*) No—please—I don't want the money—I never wanted it—don't—my heart—my... (*She suddenly keels over, gives a last strangled gasp, and then lies there, silent*)

A pause, then the ghost of Lady Chalmont moves up the stairs, rather more briskly than when she came down, and without the aid of the stick. At the same time, one of the figures lying on the floor gets up. The sound of a lever being pulled and the Lights come on. The ghost of Lady Chalmont looks down as Aurelia kneels and listens to Vera's heart. Aurelia stands, and nods

Aurelia She's gone.

The ghost of Lady Chalmont comes down the stairs and peels off the rubber face-mask. It is Mercer

Mercer What an actor. I tell you. I should have been a pro. I'd have made a fortune.

Aurelia You already have. Out of me.

Mercer (*getting out of his costume*) Don't be like that. I wouldn't do it for anyone, you know?

Aurelia Oh? Why then? Because you love me?

Mercer (*approaching her*) Something like that.

Aurelia You won't want paying then?

Mercer Give us a kiss as well. (*He tries to kiss her on the lips but she turns her cheek to him*) That's what I like about you, you're so passionate.

Aurelia I can be. And I can be a cold-hearted bitch.

Mercer Go on. You? Never.

Aurelia I know you think I'm a tart, Freddy. I'm not. I've had a few men, maybe. But only one man, at one time. I love John, whatever you may think about him. And I'm doing all this to make sure I keep him.

Mercer Don't worry about that. He won't leave you. He wouldn't dare. Still, if you're ever between husbands, and you just want a night out, think of me.

The telephone rings. Aurelia frowns, moves to answer it

Aurelia Hello, yes? Yes, Inspector.

Mercer reacts guiltily. Aurelia gestures to him not to worry

Yes, I'm well, thank you... Yes, there have been a lot of things to clear up—and I've had to look after the house, too—the housekeeper hasn't been at

Act II, Scene 2

all well—the shock of my aunt's death upset her so much—she hasn't been the same since... Yes, her heart. I keep begging her to see a doctor...

Mercer smiles, shakes his head in admiration at her coolness

News?

Aurelia is obviously shaken, and Mercer frowns

But are you sure?... You found the paintings?... And you've got a confession?... Yes, thank you... No, I'm all right. It's just so strange, knowing that you've got the murderers... It happens to you every day? It won't be more than once in my lifetime, I hope... Formal identification of the paintings? Yes, may I get my husband to call you?... No, he's not here at the moment... Tomorrow? Yes. Thank you. It was kind of you to ring ... Not at all. Good night, Inspector.

Aurelia puts down the phone, shattered. Mercer waits for an explanation

(*Drawing a deep breath*) Christ, what a fool I've been.

Mercer (*bewildered*) What..?

Aurelia (*her fury rising*) I can't believe it. I thought I was being so clever...

Mercer What the hell's happened?

Aurelia I don't know. I'm still trying to work it out. But the police have found a gang in possession of Lady Chalmont's paintings, and one of them has confessed to murdering her.

Mercer It's some nut!

Aurelia It's not one person, it's a whole gang. And they've got the paintings.

Mercer But Isabel told you——

Aurelia —a pack of bloody lies. That little cow. You'd think butter wouldn't melt in her mouth. She's been having me on, ever since she came stumbling in here, pretending she'd had a nervous breakdown...

Mercer Hold it, hold it, I'm lost. How could she pretend a thing like that and fool her doctor too? And why should she? Are you sure it wasn't her put the gang up to it?

Aurelia No. I can see what happened now. She arrived here that night and found the body. That's what put her in a state of bloody shock. But when she found out that I believed she'd done it, she just let me go on believing, told me she'd got rid of the paintings, played me along all the way—and had the bloody impertinence to demand money for it.

Mercer (*smiling*) Well. You've got to hand it to her. For an innocent little country bumpkin, that's not bad going.

Aurelia And that's not all. I wondered what the attraction was for John. I really thought it would put him off her for good, knowing she'd killed his aunt. But now I understand—she's told him she's innocent—and that means he must be in on it too—they're both conspiring against me—I'll kill them—I'll kill them both!

Mercer (*uneasily*) Hey—take it easy. I know it's a bit of a mess but...

Aurelia A bit of a mess? Don't you see I've gone through all these agonies for nothing? I didn't need you. I didn't have to kill her. (*She gestures to Vera's body*) The money was all ours, legitimately!

Mercer (*quietly*) Yours? You mean John's, don't you? (*He moves towards the door*) I'm getting out of here. Don't do anything foolish, Aurelia. Just think about it—whatever you do—and that's advice from a friend...

Aurelia does not even look at him

Mercer goes out through the garden

Aurelia looks down at the body, then out into space. Her body is trembling with hate

Aurelia You bitch! You bloody bitch!

The Lights fade to a Black-out

SCENE 3

The same. An hour later

The scene is unchanged except that Vera's body is no longer there. Aurelia sits at the desk, writing. She frowns, checks the clock, as she hears the sound of the front door closing, voices, soft laughter. The laughter, in particular, affects her, but she takes a deep breath, obviously trying to keep her temper. She rises as John and Isabel enter from the garden

Aurelia You're early.
John Yes, we didn't go to the pictures, changed our minds.
Aurelia Oh? Where did you go?
John For a drive.
Aurelia A drive?
Isabel Out in the country. To a little pub I know.
John We just had a drink and a chat.
Aurelia How cosy.
John (*refusing to rise to the bait*) Yes. It was very pleasant.
Aurelia I'm sure.
John (*niggled by her sarcasm*) Aurelia...
Isabel (*quickly*) John, don't...
Aurelia Don't what?
Isabel You're only trying to provoke us.
Aurelia Us? You're a twosome now, are you?

John is finding it hard to hold his temper. Isabel touches his arm, briefly, to remind him

Isabel I'm going to bed.
Aurelia Take him with you.
John Look, I'm warning you...
Aurelia Or have you had your ration for tonight?
John (*stepping forward*) One of these days I'll—

Act II, Scene 3

Aurelia (*sweetly*) What? Murder me? You haven't the guts.
Isabel John, it doesn't matter . . .
Aurelia (*to John*) You're not in a very sweet temper, are you? Come to think of it, I'm probably wrong. I thought you'd been having it off in the back of the car but perhaps little Miss Innocent is playing it clever, keeping you frustrated. Don't you let her get away with it. You demand your rights.
John Will you hold your filthy tongue?
Aurelia (*surprised*) Oh? You used to like talking about it. What's happened? I told you before, I don't mind what you do. You can have her here and now if you like, and I'll watch. That ought to give you a few kicks . . .

John advances on Aurelia threateningly. Isabel screams and holds on to him

Isabel (*sobbing*) John, no don't. Can't you see, she's trying to destroy you?
Aurelia (*unperturbed*) My! Listen to her! The dramatics. Mummy and Daddy must have sent her to RADA—They didn't do a very good job with her, did they?

John takes a deep breath, controls his temper. He puts an arm around Isabel to soothe her

John All right, Aurelia. That's enough. You wanted to provoke a row. You've got one. But I'm not going to fight with you. I'm not going to hit you . . .
Aurelia That's a change.
John But you wanted matters brought to a head. Fine. That suits me. Let's have it out now, once and for all.
Aurelia Go on. I'm listening. I've got no complaints, it's only you who seems upset. You and Miss untouched by human hand.
John You can sneer at this as much as you like. But I love Isabel.
Aurelia Yes?
John And she loves me.
Aurelia Well it would all be a bit pointless if it wasn't mutual. What about it?
John We're going to get married.
Aurelia Ah! Now that's not quite so simple. There are a few little obstacles in the way. Like me, for example?
John In this country, I only have to desert you and then wait.
Aurelia And what are your plans while you're waiting?
John We'll live together.
Aurelia (*mock shocked*) Isabel! What would the village say?
John We'll go away from here.
Aurelia I think you should.
John And don't try and stop us.
Aurelia What makes you think I would?

John frowns warily, suspecting a trap

What makes you think I want you any more? If that's what you want to do—maybe I'll agree—so long as you're sure . . . ?

John I'm sure.
Aurelia You could marry the girl who murdered your aunt?
John (*he blurts in out*) She didn't . . .
Aurelia (*quickly*) What?
Isabel Aurelia—it's not true—I've never told you the truth about that night. When you left me, yes, I did intend to do it. Or I think I did. I don't know now, I can't be sure. My mind was in torment. I'd always hated Lady Chalmont for sending John away, and you played on that. The shock of hearing that John was dead must have turned my mind. It didn't seem ridiculous that I should kill her because you'd suggested it to me. It was as though I was drugged, or hypnotized.

Isabel pauses, shudders, as she recalls the events of the night of the murder. Aurelia plays it as though she were quite innocent of any knowledge of what happened

Aurelia (*softly*) Yes?
Isabel I came here as we'd arranged, through the garden, having previously left the doors unlocked.
Aurelia I left them unlocked for you.
Isabel Even while I was out there, in the garden, my resolve left me. The cold air woke me as though from a dream. When I stepped in here, the revolver in my hand, I had no idea what I was going to do, but I knew I could never murder Lady Chalmont. I stood here—right here—shivering —wondering whether I should go upstairs and tell her everything—or whether I should just run away—and then suddenly I realized . . . (*She breaks off*)
Aurelia (*after a pause*) What?
Isabel That everything was strange. I don't mean the strangeness of my being there. But that the room had changed. That it was different, somehow bare. And then I saw the paintings had gone.
Aurelia What are you trying to say? That someone had been here before you?
Isabel It's true. I swear it. I know it's the most bizarre coincidence that anyone could think up, but it does have a kind of logic. We did know that there had been burglaries in the area.
Aurelia (*harshly*) But not murder.
Isabel No. I left the revolver here, went upstairs. Lady Chalmont's door was open. She was lying there, in a pool of blood. (*She sobs*) It was horrible. (*Taking control of herself*) But my mind was suddenly crystal clear. I came down again, picked up the gun. I went to the river and got rid of it, just as you'd instructed me. I went back home and got in to my room without anyone seeing me. (*In a whisper*) I went to sleep that night like a weary child, as though I'd done nothing but play all day—(*a pause*) —and the next thing I knew, when I woke up, was that it was three days later, and I'd been delirious, but just apparently playing out some nightmare of my youth. So far as I know, I never said a word about our plans.
Aurelia (*with a shrug*) Well that's a pretty tall story.
Isabel I swear it's what happened. As soon as I could, I came here to tell

Act II, Scene 3   57

you, to explain, but I never had a chance. You confused my mind by telling me that Mercer never existed, for a while I really thought I'd gone mad, and when John appeared, I was sure I had.
John That was her plan, I bet.
Aurelia Never mind my plans, let's talk about Isabel's. Because even if I believe your story, and it takes some believing, that still leaves a few questions to be answered.
Isabel You mean why I acted the way I did? Because I wanted revenge, I suppose. I don't know how long I was out when I fainted. I suppose it could only have been a couple of minutes. I do know that I heard your conversation while I was supposed to be unconscious. And that's when I decided to demand the money and make you—both of you—suffer a little at least as I had done. It was as though, having been the victim, I wanted to be the executioner for a change.
Aurelia I see. And why are you telling me now?
Isabel Because this is an important conversation. Let's make it an honest one.
John You'd have tried to blackmail Isabel, to stop us going off. Well now you can't. She's innocent of Aunt Margaret's death.
Aurelia We're all innocent, aren't we? If her story's true. No-one's got anything on anyone.
John That's right. It's best that way.
Aurelia Is it?
Isabel John and I have talked it over, Aurelia. You can have his inheritance. We don't want it. We'd rather start fresh.
Aurelia And clean. And virginal.
John *(suddenly, in a hard voice)* Do you want it or not?
Aurelia Well of course, I worked hard enough for it. But how are you going to manage?
John I'll find a job.
Aurelia That's a laugh.
Isabel And I'll work too.
Aurelia That sounds more like it.
John You don't have to keep sneering.
Aurelia I'm not sneering. Just a little sceptical. What happens when a baby comes along.
John *(embracing Isabel)* We want a family.
Aurelia There are family allowances over here, of course. But it would take an awful lot of them to keep you in the style you like to live.
John You can mock at us as much as you like. We've made up our minds. And we knew just how you'd react.
Aurelia Did you?
Isabel Don't try and stop us, Aurelia.
Aurelia *(after a pause)* You don't really think I'd let you go, do you? Just like that?
John Please. I beg you. Don't make any more trouble.
Aurelia I love you.
John Then let me go.

Aurelia With her?
John Yes.
Aurelia Do I have a choice?
John None. Except to take it well—or badly.

There is a pause. Aurelia turns away. She does not reply

Isabel John. Let's go now. Tonight.

Aurelia takes a deep breath, turns to face them

Aurelia All right.
John What?
Aurelia Go.

John and Isabel exchange glances, unable to believe it

Isabel D'you mean it?
Aurelia Yes.
John Do you?
Aurelia What the hell—there's nothing to be gained by making a fuss—and you were always a—oh, let her have the problem.

Aurelia moves over to the drinks tray, starts to pour herself a drink

John Aurelia—if you mean it—I'm grateful.
Aurelia That's a backhanded compliment. I can't work that one out. You're grateful that—perhaps I'd better not try and work it out. (*She pours more drinks*) Here—let's all drink on it. (*Aurelia carries their drinks across to them, then goes back for her own glass*) I'm not going to wish you all the good luck in the world—that would be hypocritical. But I won't wish you any bad luck either.
John It's the best way, Aurelia. There's no need to be bitter.
Isabel I hope things work out for you, Aurelia, whatever way you want.
Aurelia I'll drink to that.

They all drink. There is a moment of awkward silence

Where are you going? To London?
John (*looking at Isabel*) I suppose so.
Isabel They'll all talk in the village, but I suppose it can't be helped.
Aurelia (*with a shrug*) It won't worry me. I'll say John had to fly back to Africa. Let them work out for themselves where you've disappeared to.
Isabel I'll say I got a job in a library in London.
Aurelia How are you going? By the late train?
John I suppose that's best.
Aurelia Leave the keys in the car, in the station yard. I'll pick it up tomorrow.
John O.K. (*He glances at his watch*) I'd better pack some things.
Isabel I won't take anything, except what I've got here. I can get them to send my things on later.
John (*moving to the stairs*) Will you, er . . .?
Aurelia John, do me a favour, just go, before I change my mind. And leave Isabel here. I want to talk to her.

Act II, Scene 3

John looks a bit alarmed

It's all right. I'm not going to reveal all the skeletons in your cupboard. It's just female chat.

John looks at Isabel for reassurance. Isabel smiles at him

Isabel You go on up. Pack. I'll stay here and talk to Aurelia. Then when you're ready, we'll leave.
John *(a trifle uneasily)* O.K.

John exits upstairs

As John disappears from view, the two women look at each other. Aurelia smiles, raises her glass, drinks. Isabel drinks as well

Aurelia You know, I hope things do work out for you. But John's a risk, you know. He's weak, and easily led.
Isabel I'll risk it.
Aurelia There've been other girls.
Isabel I know. He's told me.
Aurelia Everything?
Isabel Everything.
Aurelia Well—you've got guts . . .
Isabel No. Just a quiet confidence. I've known him much longer than you have, remember, even though you are his wife.
Aurelia *(after a pause)* I loved him. I really loved him.
Isabel Yes. But . . .
Aurelia What?
Isabel It's not for me to say. Except I think love should be giving—not encircling, suffocating . . .
Aurelia Is that how it was for John with me?
Isabel I . . . *(she does not know what to say)*

Aurelia turns away. Isabel is upset that she has been cruel

I'm sorry.
Aurelia Don't be.
Isabel *(after a pause)* What will you do?
Aurelia *(flatly)* Kill myself.
Isabel *(forcing a smile)* You don't mean that.
Aurelia Why not? Oh, don't worry, I won't involve you two. I'll leave a note, saying that I had a morbid suspicion I was suffering from some incurable disease . . .
Isabel But there's no need. You've got your whole life ahead of you. You're beautiful and attractive to men—you've got money . . .
Aurelia That's the big problem about loving, isn't it? We all love what we can't have. And the people who love us are the ones we don't want. There's such a lot of love in the world and it's so bloody unevenly divided out. You'd think it would be a simple thing, wouldn't you, for some heavenly computer to work out, just for A to be matched with B, and C with D, and so on. *(She moves to the drinks tray)* Hell, let's have another drink . . .

Isabel (*swaying slightly*) No—not for me, thanks—I've only had a couple but—I suppose it's all the excitement—I feel quite faint.

Aurelia (*pouring herself a drink*) Something exciting going on around here? Nobody told me. (*She comes back to Isabel*) So you're feeling a bit woozey, are you? Well, before I run and get the smelling salts for you, you listen to me, you bitch, and listen to me good. It's not all as clean and neat as you would like it be. We happen still to have a corpse to get rid of.

Isabel (*aghast, struggling to hold on to consciousness*) What?

Aurelia Yes. You weren't the only one trying to take me for a ride. Obviously every bumpkin in the country decided I was a sucker as soon as I moved in—(*she moves to the dining-room door to open it*)—including this one ... (*She opens the door*)

Vera is propped up, just inside. As Aurelia tugs her shoulder, Vera falls into the room

Isabel Vera!

Aurelia Yes. I decided to sell up and dispose of my staff. And I intend to dispose of you, too, Miss Goody-two-shoes. In my own subtle and inimitable way.

Isabel (*staggering, holding on to a chair for support*) You've poisoned me!

Aurelia Darling! You're always so dramatic! I've done nothing of the kind. It's just a small overdose of my sleeping pills. You can't notice the bitterness in alcohol, can you?

Isabel tries to make it to the stairs. She calls out but her voice is strangled

Isabel John—John!

But her cry is little more than a whisper. As she gets to the foot of the stairs, she collapses. Eyes glazed, she watches as Aurelia, smiling, dials a number on the telephone. At the same time, Aurelia takes a revolver from the desk drawer, points it at Isabel

Aurelia (*breathlessly*) Inspector Briggs please. (*She acts like mad when the Inspector comes on the phone*) Hello, Inspector, this is Aurelia Chalmont. Will you please come here at once—someone's threatening to kill me ... Yes, *kill* me—aaaaaaahhhh! Don't—please ...!

Isabel's eyes close. Aurelia, who has the gun pointed at her, lifts it to the ceiling and fires two shots. She lets the phone dangle from the hook, first cutting it off. Then she points the gun again at Isabel

John comes rushing down the stairs

John Oh, my God ...

Aurelia (*pointing the gun at him*) She's dead, John. And now it's your turn.

John, at the foot of the stairs, gasps as he sees Vera's body

Yes, her too. I told you I wouldn't let her get away with blackmailing me.

John (*sobbing*) You're mad. Mad!

Aurelia Yes. I am. I must have been to give up everything I had for you. You lied to me, cheated me, but still I went on loving you. If that's not

Act II, Scene 3

raving mad, to be passionately in love with a weak, no-good, stupid son-of-a-bitch like you, what is? But love's got no reason about it, Johnny, it makes you mad. I wasn't ever going to let you run away with that bitch. (*She advances towards him*) And now she's dead. And you've got to stay with me. Or I'll kill you here and now. Do you understand? I'll kill you . . .

Aurelia suddenly breaks down, sobbing. Her gun-hand drops and John grabs her wrist, wrests the gun from her. He takes a pace back from Aurelia, aims the gun at her

John She was all I ever wanted, always. If my aunt hadn't always been pushing me towards what she thought were better things, we'd have been all right. I married you because I thought I'd never ever see Isabel again but —when I did—I knew that nothing had changed, not for us. She was the only person who understood me, ever, who knew me for what I really was . . .

Aurelia A cheap no-good crook. A tuppeny halfpenny philanderer. A weak nothing.

John Shut up, or I'll murder you.

Aurelia You haven't got the guts. You never have had. You never will have. I can shoot the great love of your life, your darling Isabel, cold stone dead, and you haven't even got the guts to pull the trigger . . .

John fires. Once. Twice. Three times. Aurelia's body jerks with the impact of each bullet. She crawls downstage. He stares down at her, horrified

Thank you, baby. I knew you wouldn't let me down. That was all I wanted. I'm tired of this life. I wanted to leave it. But I wasn't going to leave you behind to enjoy life, at my expense. I never killed Isabel. She's fine—just a little drugged, that's all—but you try explaining that to the police. They'll be here any time now. Poor Vera. She saw you go mad and kill your wife for love of your mistress. It gave her a heart attack . . .

John stares at her for a moment, aghast. He crosses quickly to Isabel, checks that she is indeed alive, and then moves to Vera. He sees that Vera is dead. He looks across at Aurelia, then presses the gun in Vera's hand. He moves across to Aurelia, kneels by her

John No, Aurelia. You've got it wrong. Poor Vera, who has been demented since dear Lady Chalmont's death, shot you and then had a heart attack. Isabel, who has had one nervous breakdown promptly had another. I'm the only witness who can give a good account of it—and I'll give a very good account, my darling, even though I am heartbroken.

Aurelia (*with a faint smile*) You bastard—I made you just like me . . .

John (*with sudden compassion*) Why all this, Aurelia why . . .?

Aurelia (*in pain now*) Because—I'm—me . . . (*She closes her eyes against the final pain of her death*)

The sound of police sirens is heard approaching. John moves across to cradle Isabel. He looks across at his dead wife, as—

the CURTAIN *falls*

FURNITURE AND PROPERTY LIST

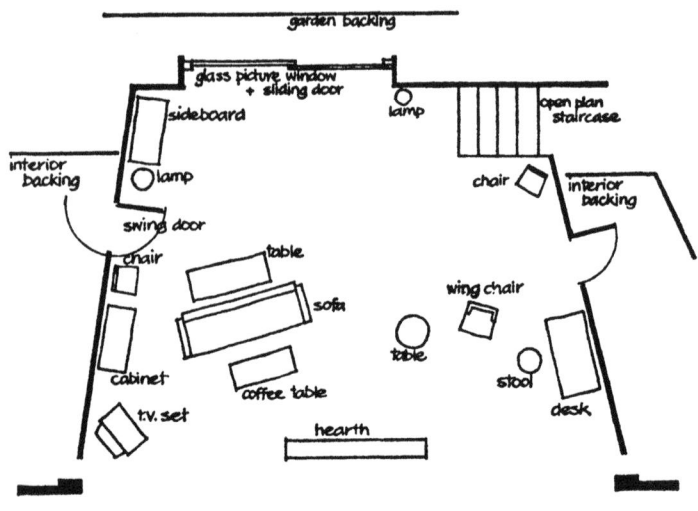

ACT 1

Scene 1

On stage: Sofa
Sofa table. *On it:* lamp, cigarettes in box, ashtray, lighter
Coffee table
Wing-chair
2 small chairs
Occasional table
Desk. *On it:* lamp, writing materials, note pad, telephone, **Lady Chalmont's** handbag with letter
Desk stool
Cabinet. *On it:* clock, tray with sherry, glasses. *Inside:* photograph album
Sideboard. *In it:* bottle of brandy
2 standard lamps
T. V. set
On walls: collection of paintings, mirror
On furniture: assorted ornaments
Carpet
Stair carpet
Window curtains

Off stage: Dishcloth (**Vera**)

Aurelia

Tea-tray with 2 cups, 2 saucers, 2 teaspoons, sugar bowl, milk jug, plate of cakes, biscuits (Vera)
Teapot, full (Vera)
Cup, saucer, teaspoon (Vera)
String bag with books (Isabel)
Bottle of pills (Vera)

Personal: Mrs Chalmont: walking-stick

Scene 2

Strike: Tea-tray
Books
Pills
Lady Chalmont's handbag

Set: Several travelling cases on floor. *In one:* wrapped parcel containing necklace, wrapped parcel containing African mask
Glass door open

Off stage: Vase of flowers (Vera)
Bar of soap (Vera)
Overseas telegram (Vera)

Scene 3

Strike: Vase of flowers
Remaining cases
Necklace and wrapping
Mask and wrapping
Dirty glasses
Telegram

Set: Tray back on drinks cabinet

Off stage: Tray with jug of chocolate and 3 cups (Vera)
Overnight case (Vera)
Plate of biscuits (Vera)
Revolver (Mercer)

Personal: Aurelia: pill box in handbag

Scene 4

Strike: Dirty glasses
Chocolate tray, cups, biscuits
All paintings, some ornaments

Set: Photo album back in cabinet

Off stage: Tray with coffee pot, sugar bowl, cup, saucer, spoon

ACT II
Scene 1

Off stage: Smelling salts (Vera)

Scene 2

Strike: Dirty glasses

Set: Television set out a little into room
On *coffee table:* 2 large plates, 2 small plates, 2 forks (all used), 2 coffee cups, 2 saucers

Off stage: Plate of food, with fork (Vera)
Lady Chalmont's stick (Mercer)
Revolver (Mercer)
Rubber face-mask (Mercer)

Personal: **John:** wristwatch
Aurelia: wristwatch

Scene 3

Set: Revolver in desk drawer

LIGHTING PLOT

Property fittings required: table lamp, desk lamp, 2 standard lamps, porch light, television effect
Interior. A drawing-room. The same scene throughout

ACT I, SCENE 1. Day
To open: Effect of dull, rainy March afternoon
Cue 1   Isabel reads letter   (Page 9)
          Fade to spot on Isabel, then to Black-out

ACT I, SCENE 2. Day
To open: Effect of bright sunshine
Cue 2   **Isabel** replaces phone   (Page 17)
          Fade to spot on Isabel, then to Black-out

ACT I, SCENE 3. Night
To open: Room in darkness, porch light on, moonlight effect in garden
Cue 3   **Aurelia** and **Isabel** turn on lights   (Page 17)
          *Snap on both standard lamps, desk and table lamps, and
          covering spots, to coincide*
Cue 4   **Aurelia** switches off one **standard lamp**   (Page 30)
          Snap off one standard lamp and covering spot
Cue 5   **Aurelia** switches off table lamp and second standard lamp   (Page 30)
          *Snap off table lamp and second standard lamp and covering
          spots—leaving desk lamp and porch light*
Cue 6   **Aurelia** switches on standard lamp   (Page 30)
          Snap on one standard lamp and covering spot
Cue 7   **Aurelia** switches on table lamp   (Page 31)
          Snap on table lamp and covering spot
Cue 8   **Aurelia**: "What's happened to you?"   (Page 34)
          Fade to spot on Isabel, then to Black-out

ACT I, SCENE 4. Day
To open: Black-out
Cue 9   After glass crash   (Page 34)
          Fade up to effect of sunny morning

ACT II, SCENE 1. Day
To open: As close of Act I, Scene 4
Cue 10   **Aurelia:** "Isabel—Mercer—Vera . . ."   (Page 46)
             Fade to Black-out

ACT II, SCENE 2. Night
To open: All interior lighting on. T.V. set on
Cue 11   **John** switches off T.V.   (Page 49)
             Fade television light
Cue 12   **Vera:** ". . . a card, you really are . . ."   (Page 51)
             Snap out all interior lighting, retain watery moon effect in garden
Cue 13   **As Mercer** pulls mains switch   (Page 52)
             Return to opening lighting
Cue 14   **Aurelia:** "You bloody bitch!"   (Page 54)
             Fade to Black-out

ACT II, SCENE 3. Night
To open: As opening of Scene
No cues

EFFECTS PLOT

ACT I

SCENE 1

Cue 1	**Lady Chalmont:** ". . . calls for any aha's?" *Kettle whistles*	(Page 2)
Cue 2	After **Vera** exits *Kettle whistle stops*	(Page 2)

SCENE 2

Cue 3	**Vera:** ". . . what people will say." *Telephone rings*	(Page 14)
Cue 4	**Vera:** ". . . will be in twenty minutes." *Front doorbell rings*	(Page 15)
Cue 5	**Lady Chalmont:** "Thank you." *Telephone rings*	(Page 16)

SCENE 3

Cue 6	After CURTAIN rises *Sound of car driving up, stopping, doors slamming*	(Page 17)
Cue 7	**Isabel:** "You're always so thoughtful." *Car hooter sounds*	(Page 22)

SCENE 4

Cue 8	At start of scene *Three shots, then glass crash*	(Page 34)
Cue 9	After Lights come up *Sound of car driving up, stopping, doors slamming*	(Page 34)
Cue 10	**Aurelia:** "That might be nice." *Telephone rings*	(Page 36)

ACT II

SCENE 1

No cues

SCENE 2

Cue 11	As CURTAIN rises *TV programme from set, very low volume*	(Page 46)

Cue 12	**John** switches T.V. off *Television programme fades*	(Page 49)
Cue 13	**Mercer** (as ghost) returns upstairs *Sound of mains light switch being pulled*	(Page 52)
Cue 14	**Mercer:** ". . . think of me." *Telephone rings*	(Page 52)

SCENE 3

Cue 15	**Aurelia:** ". . . Because—I'm—me . . ." *Sound of police siren approaching*	(Page 61)

www.ingramcontent.com/pod-product-compliance
Ingram Content Group UK Ltd.
Pitfield, Milton Keynes, MK11 3LW, UK
UKHW021846210426
5322IPUK00022B/499